THE CHRONICALLY
MENTALLY ILL

THE CHRONICALLY MENTALLY ILL:
Assessing Community Support Programs

RICHARD C. TESSLER, Ph. D.
Associate Professor
Department of Sociology
University of Massachusetts
Amherst, Massachusetts

HOWARD H. GOLDMAN, M.D., M.P.H., Ph.D.
Assistant Professor of Psychiatry
Langley Porter Psychiatric Institute
University of California
San Francisco, California

and Associates

Ballinger Publishing Company
Cambridge, Massachusetts
A Subsidiary of Harper & Row, Publishers, Inc.

International Standard Book Number: 0-88410-379-X

Library of Congress Catalog Card Number: 82-3884

Printed in the United States of America

Library of Congress Cataloging in Publication Data

Tessler, Richard C.
   The chronically mentally ill.

   Includes bibliographies and index.
   1. Community mental health services—United States—
Evaluation. I. Goldman, Howard H. II. Title.
RA790.6.T48   362.2'0425'0973   82-3884
ISBN 0-88410-379-X   AACR2

Table of Contents

LIST OF FIGURES

LIST OF TABLES

PREFACE

The history of the care of the mentally ill may be characterized as a series of cycles of neglect and reform. Each cycle of reform was marked by optimism that a new institution or form of treatment would solve the problem of mental illness and transcend the failures of the past. The asylum and moral treatment replaced the jail, the almshouse, and community neglect. The psychopathic hospital and clinics and the mental hygiene movement replaced the overcrowded, underfunded asylum. The community mental health center and movement tried to prevent mental disorder, replace state mental hospitals, and return patients home. Each reform hoped to treat new, acute cases and prevent chronicity, but each was unsuccessful in that regard.

Beginning in the mid-1970s, a new conceptual model emerged for improving the quality of life of the chronically mentally ill. Derived from theories and research indicating the significance of social support networks in the course of mental disorder, the model assumes that a natural support system, bolstered by a network of services, can ameliorate the stress of adjustment to community life. As adapted by the National Institute of Mental Health (NIMH) Community Support Program (CSP), the model specified ten essential components for comprehensive care. These ten components extended beyond the boundaries of the mental health service agencies. At the state level, a special CSP unit was established which would assess the needs of the target population and lobby for the statewide interests of the chronically mentally ill. At the local level, a core service agency that would take responsibility for securing and integrating all ten service components in order to create a genuine community support system was to be designated. At the client-patient level, an individual person (or team) was to remain in contact with the client-patient on a continuing basis in order to assure that each client was receiving appropriate services.

CSP offers a new reform. Instead of seeking to prevent mental disorder, CSP wishes to provide a "network of caring" for the chronically mentally ill living in community settings, based upon a diversity of health, mental health, rehabilitation, and social welfare services. Does CSP represent a fourth cycle of reform? What are its initial successes? What are its shortcomings and problems for the future?

The chapters that follow describe CSP and provide an initial assessment. Designed to provide community based services and social support for the noninstitutionalized chronically mentally ill, CSP became the model for many states, for the Mental Health Systems Act (MHSA), and for programs to be developed under block grants. Ideally, it would be possible to evaluate this program's impact on systems of care at the state level, on local services, and on the individual client-patient. What follows is more limited. While issues pertinent to program impact are raised in the following chapters, most of the data presented are descriptive. However, the descriptive material does point the way toward future studies.

The book is divided into four parts. Part I defines the scope of the problem from an epidemiological and historical perspective, and describes how the initial assessment of CSP was planned and implemented during the program's formative years. The evaluation activities reviewed encompass an array of efforts geared to the program, client, and system levels of analysis. Part II of the book addresses the program level of evaluation. Separate chapters in this section assess the logic of the program, its plausibility, and the implementation of state programs.

Part III, addressed to the client level of analysis, includes chapters describing client characteristics and use of services, and factors affecting adjustment to community living. Part IV, the concluding part of the book, focuses on the larger system of mental health and other human services. Separate chapters assess the potential need for community supports and discuss methodologies appropriate to the assessment of interorganizational linkages and system development at the local level. A concluding chapter summarizes evaluation findings from prior chapters, assesses their implications, and addresses public policy issues surrounding the future of CSPs in the United States.

In writing this book, we have drawn on our experiences at NIMH as staff members of the Division of Biometry and Epidemiology. However, the actual writing occurred after we had left the federal government, and reflects the particular vantage point of two academics—one in a department of sociology and the other in a department of psychiatry. As authors of this book, we see ourselves as both sympathetic "insiders" and as skeptical "outsiders." We hope that this dual perspective has enriched our assessment of the NIMH program and, more generally, of the needs of the chronically mentally ill.

The book represents a joint effort undertaken in collaboration with several persons who made important contributions to CSP evaluation. Two of these colleagues, Joseph Morrissey and John Ashbaugh, contributed original chapters for this book (see Chapters 8 and 9). Three others, Alice Bernstein, Beatrice Rosen, and Ronald Manderscheid, contributed as coauthors (see Chapters 6 and 7). We also acknowledge the contributions of Macro Systems, Inc., a consulting firm in Silver Spring, Maryland, upon whose work we drew in preparing the program-analysis chapters (see Chapters 3, 4, and 5). From Macro Systems, Inc., we thank Martin Kotler, Lanny Morrisson, Beth Stroul, Tal Ben Dashan, and Phyllis Rienzo.

Condensed versions of Chapters 6 and 7 have been previously published. We thank *Hospital & Community Psychiatry* for permission to reproduce material from "The Chronically Mentally Ill in Community Support Systems" (33, no. 3, March: 208–211) and "Factors Affecting Adjustment to Community Living" (33, no. 3, March: 203–207).

Our work on CSP evaluation was performed with the participation and support of many government colleagues in the NIMH and other offices within the Department of Health and Human

Services: Paul Carling, Antoinette Gattozzi, Sam Keith, Robert Lilly, Janet Meleney, David Pharis, Darrel Regier, Jacqueline Rosenberg, John Sessler, Steven Sharfstein, Irene Shifren, Jerry Storck, Robert Washington, and J. Richard Woy. We give special thanks to Judith Turner, the CSP branch chief, for her receptivity to evaluation and for her critical perspective. Similarly, we thank CSP staff in state and local projects whose cooperation made this book possible. We appreciate the energy of our typists, Susan Elliott, Randy Griffin, Chris Hall, and Sally Ives, the careful proofreading by Mary-Louise Creekmore, and the support of our families. Finally, we thank Carol Franco and Steven Cramer, our editors at Ballinger Publishing Company, and Joseph Morrissey of the New York State Office of Mental Health, who encouraged this project from its beginning and who generously shared his ideas with us during critical points in the book's development.

RCT and HHG
March 1982

A NETWORK OF CARING

1 THE SCOPE OF THE PROBLEM

This is a book about a National Institute of Mental Health (NIMH) initiative on behalf of the chronically mentally ill living in community settings throughout the United States. The initiative, known as the Community Support Program (CSP), represents a long-awaited federal response to the problems and challenges posed by the deinstitutionalization of the chronically mentally ill. Reflecting this new federal commitment, the CSP model was incorporated into the Mental Health Systems Act (MHSA), which was signed into law in October 1980. With this new legislation, CSP appeared to be poised on the brink of being transformed into a major mental health service program.

Soon thereafter, the political environment for federally financed mental health services, and for human services more generally, changed radically, and with it, so have the prospects and challenges facing CSP. The MHSA, which was to provide the authority and resources for CSP's transformation, has been repealed almost entirely. The federal human service budget has been slashed substantially. The advent of block grants and the "new federalism" of the Reagan administration are pointing to a basic shift in the locus of power and authority from federal to state government. Mirroring these changes in the political environment, NIMH is anticipating a greatly diminished role in the delivery of mental health services through categorical programs.

For better or worse, the new federalism of the 1980s confronts CSP with a critical test. Can CSPs continue to thrive without substantial categorical support from the federal government? Is CSP "an idea whose time has come," or is it merely the latest cycle of reform in a series of abortive attempts to deal responsibly with the problem of chronic mental disability?

While the test may be premature and the conditions trying, it does provide the opportunity to test the viability of the CSP model independent of federal influence and control.[1] Considering the fierce competition for scarce resources at the state level, and the absence of powerful constituencies ready to advocate for the special interests of the chronically mentally ill, the growth of CSPs would be remarkable. By the same token, failure of CSP to thrive under current conditions should not lead to a wholesale rejection of the model. Neither should the leadership role of NIMH be discounted. The federal CSP initiative has provided a creative laboratory to assess and give national visibility to a particular configuration of principles and services.

This book describes the federal CSP and its initial assessment. Before discussing CSP in detail, we will outline the scope of the problem of chronic mental disability from an epidemiological and historical perspective.

WHO ARE THE CHRONICALLY MENTALLY ILL?

There is much controversy surrounding use of the term "chronically mentally ill." The emphasis on chronicity strikes some observers as being overly pessimistic and promoting a self-fulfilling prognosis. Others view the term "mentally ill" as pejorative and stigmatizing. They feel that such language represents an inappropriate application of the medical disease model. Recognizing this controversy, we nonetheless use the term "chronically mentally ill" because it is in common use and is easily understood.

In this book, we use the terms "client" and "patient" interchangeably, reflecting both the social and medical elements of the CSP. Because the NIMH CSP uses the term "client," we most often adopt this phraseology. Although CSP is a broad social program, its clients are also psychiatric patients in need of specialized health and mental health services.

Target Population   At about the same time that the MHSA was first being considered by the Congress, A National Plan for the Chronically Mentally Ill (NP/CMI) was being developed by a coalition of federal agencies within the Department of Health and Human Services in response to the President's Commission on Mental Health (1978). As an early planning step, the NP/CMI provided an operational definition and a count of the target population. Utilizing a three-dimensional concept based on diagnosis, disability, and duration, the NP/CMI (1980:2–11) stated:

> The chronically mentally ill population encompasses persons who suffer certain mental or emotional disorders (organic brain syndrome, schizophrenia, recurrent depressive and manic-depressive disorders, and paranoid and other psychoses, plus other disorders that may become chronic) that erode or prevent the development of their functional capacities in relation to three or more primary aspects of daily life—personal hygiene and self-care, self-direction, interpersonal relationships, social transactions, learning, and recreation—and that erode or prevent the development of their economic self-sufficiency.
>
> Most such individuals have required institutional care of extended duration, including intermediate-term hospitalization (90 days to 365 days in a single year), long-term hospitalization (one year or longer in the preceding five years), or nursing home placement because of a diagnosed mental condition or a diagnosis of senility without psychosis. Some such individuals have required short-term hospitalization (less than 90 days); others have received treatment from a medical or mental health professional solely on an outpatient basis, or—despite their needs—have received no treatment in the professional service system. Thus included in the target population are persons who are or were formerly residents of institutions (public and private psychiatric hospitals and nursing homes) and persons who are at high risk of institutionalization because of persistent mental disability.

The complexity of this definition reflects the heterogeneity of the population and suggests the difficulty encountered in determining its magnitude. Estimates developed for the plan (Goldman, Gattozzi, and Taube 1981) place the size of the population at between 1.7 and 2.4 million Americans. As Table 1–1 indicates, this population includes 900,000 who are institutionalized in mental health facilities and nursing homes, 800,000 who reside in the community and are severely disabled, and an additional 700,000 in the community who are moderately disabled.

The NP/CMI recommended a series of service and training programs and urged policy changes in major federal programs, including those authorized by the Social Security Act (Titles II, XVI, XVIII, XIX, XX) and the Rehabilitation Services Act. The NP/CMI, which represented a major commitment of federal time and effort directed toward the interest of a multiply handicapped and neglected population, stalled on the desk of the lame duck secretary of the Department of Health and Human Services. On January 19, 1981, the last day of the Carter Administration, it was finally released as a "working document" and not departmental policy. Its recommendations remain controversial, reflecting myriad concerns surrounding the care of the chronically mentally ill.

The following section reviews the history of social policy toward the chronically mentally ill in America. The review serves as a background for the more detailed story of the CSP, a model for both the MHSA and the NP/CMI and NIMH's major initiative in the care of the chronically mentally ill in the community.

Table 1-1.   Estimates of the Number of Chronically Mentally Ill (Unduplicated Counts), United States, 1975–1977.

Setting	Population (range)	
	Low	High
Institution		
Mental health facilities	150,000	150,000
Nursing homes		
Mental disorder	350,000	350,000
Senility without psychosis	400,000	400,000
Subtotal	900,000	900,000
Community		
Severely disabled	800,000	800,000
Moderately disabled	——	700,000
Subtotal	800,000	1,500,000
Total	1,700,000	2,400,000

Source: Goldman, Gattozzi, and Taube. (1981: 24).

CYCLES OF REFORM

The history of the care of the chronically mentally ill in America has been described as a series of cycles of alternating neglect and reform associated with changes in the locus of care (Morrissey, Goldman, and Klerman 1980; Dain 1980). Each reform has focused on a new environmental approach to the treatment of the mentally ill and has championed an innovative type of facility or network of services. Each cycle began with the promise of early treatment of mental disorder in a new setting which would prevent long-term disability. Each reform met with early success in the treatment of acute cases but ultimately failed to prevent chronicity and failed to alter fundamentally the care of the severely mentally ill. In fact, in each cycle, early optimism faded into disappointment over the increasing numbers of patients who were incurable. These "chronic cases" represented the failure of the reform. As chronic patients accumulated in acute-treatment settings or returned to the community, they drew heavily upon resources originally allocated for acute-treatment services. The resulting scarcity of resources, coupled with disappointment over the inability to meet exaggerated expectations, led to a period of pessimism, retrenchment, and neglect—especially of the chronically ill.

In the United States, there have been at least three major reform movements and reform institutions. Each has been described elsewhere in considerable detail. The first cycle of reform introduced moral treatment and the asylum (Grob 1966, 1973; Caplan 1969), the second cycle generated the mental hygiene movement and the psychopathic hospital (Rothman 1980), and the third reform created the community mental health movement and the community mental health center (Joint Commission 1961; Levinson and Brown 1967). In turn, each movement and its special facility flourished and then faltered. A fourth reform, associated with psychosocial rehabilitation and community support systems (CSSs) has developed within the community mental health movement and has spawned several programs at the state and local levels. The NIMH CSP has been the focus of federal efforts to address the needs of the chronically mentally ill in the community. In its own words, it is a "pilot approach to a needed social reform" (Turner and TenHoor 1978). Before examining the current reform movement, let us look as the previous cycles of reform to provide a historical context.

Moral Treatment and the Asylum   Exported from Europe to America in the late eighteenth and early nineteenth century, moral treatment was based on the concept that new cases of insanity could be cured by segregating the "distracted" into asylums where they would receive humane care and instruction. Adopted first in America by private institutions like the McLean Asylum and the Hartford Retreat, moral treatment was soon advocated for use in public institutions by social reformers like Horace Mann and Dorothea Dix. Their efforts to establish and expand the Lunatic Asylum at Worcester (Mass.) soon led to the rapid proliferation of public asylums throughout Jacksonian America (Grob 1966, 1973; Rothman 1971; Morrissey, Goldman, and Klerman 1980). By the 1850s, almost as soon as they became well established, asylums were becoming overcrowded with chronic cases. The claims of 100 percent cures were overstated. Actually, the early asylums experienced approximately 60 percent recovery rates—comparable to modern figures, but far below the expectations created by early proponents of moral treatment (Bockoven 1972). The public became disillusioned and began to withdraw fiscal support. As the asylum grew larger and continued to operate with fixed resources, the quality of care and treatment deteriorated. By the late 1860s and 1870s, hospitals developed chronic-care divisions and separate asylums for the chronically insane (Grob 1973).

One notable exception to this trend was the proposal to build small cottages to replace large centralized institutions. Originally suggested in the 1850s by John Galt, superintendent of the State Asylum at Williamsburg, Virginia, this proposal was ressurrected after the Civil War by Merrick Bemis, superintendent at the Worcester Asylum (Dain 1980). Bemis became embroiled in a controversy over his proposal to develop a cottage-type hospital. Opposed by fellow superintendents and by conservative members of the legislature, the cottage plan was defeated. Bemis resigned and a large centralized institution for the chronically mentally ill was built at Worcester (Grob 1966).

The rise of pathological anatomy supported the pessimistic notion that mental illness was a chronic, organic disease from which

there was little hope of recovery. This therapeutic nihilism signaled the end of the era of moral treatment. The small, pastoral
asylum of hope and humane care had become a large, monolithic
repository of human suffering and despair.

*The Mental Hygiene Movement and the Psychopathic Hospi-
tal*   The pessimism of pathological anatomy gave way to the optimism of a scientific psychiatry associated with turn-of-the-
century figures such as Adolf Meyer and William James. The
work of these brilliant scientists, reinforced by the development
of psychoanalysis, restored hope that the mentally ill could be
effectively treated. The public was outraged by exposés of conditions in mental hospitals, but the 1908 publication of *A Mind
That Found Itself,* Clifford Beers' account of his experiences as a
mental patient, added a note of optimism to the prevailing criti-
cism.

In 1909, Beers sought the support of Meyer and James to help
him found the National Committee for Mental Hygiene. This reform organization revived the notion of the treatability of mental
disorder, especially by early intervention with acute cases. The
reformists advocated creating a "psychopathic hospital," an
acute-treatment center associated with training and research institutions. Building upon the earlier concept of moral treatment
and several later innovations in psychiatric care, psychopathic
hospitals opened in Ann Arbor, Baltimore, and Boston (Rothman
1980). The reform spread and spawned other new mental health
agencies such as psychiatric dispensaries and child-guidance clinics. However, these new facilities were unable to eliminate chronic
illness. They provided high-quality care for a few but were unable
to fundamentally reform American mental health care. In the absence of specific treatments, mental disorders remained chronic
illnesses and mental hospitals remained predominantly chronic-
care facilities providing long-term custody of the poor and disabled (Dain 1980; Rothman 1980; Grob 1973; Deutsch 1948).

*The Community Mental Health Movement and the Community
Mental Health Center*   World War II simultaneously marked the
nadir in the decline of the enthusiasm surrounding the mental
health hygiene movement and the turning point initiating the
third cycle of reform. The finding that so many young Americans

were mentally unfit for military duty, coupled with the front line successes of brief interventions in the treatment of "war neurosis," stimulated renewed interest in mental health and new optimism for the treatment of mental illness. The community mental health movement was born out of this enthusiasm for brief treatment techniques which avoided the removal of patients to faraway hospitals (Joint Commission 1961). The returning military psychiatrists experimented with brief hospitalization and new psychosocial treatment techniques, and by the mid-1950s, made extensive use of the new psychotropic medications (Milbank 1962). In the late 1940s and early 1950s, pioneer mental health professionals, like Erich Lindemann, adapted new techniques in brief therapy and psychiatric consultation for use in outpatient clinics, creating mental health centers in the community (Mora 1967). At the same time, innovative mental hospitals opened after-care clinics to serve increasing numbers of discharged mental patients (Milbank 1962) and general hospitals opened acute psychiatric inpatient units (Linn 1961). Again, reformers offered the promise that early intervention in a community setting could prevent chronicity and long-term disability, rendering the mental hospital obsolete.

In 1946, the National Mental Health Act had created the NIMH and the Joint Commission on Mental Illness and Health. The final report of the Joint Commission, *Action for Mental Health*, (1961) promoted the concept of community mental health care. This concept became the "bold new approach" adopted by President Kennedy in the Community Mental Health Centers Act, which created the elaborate system of community mental health centers (CMHCs) in the mid-1960s.

Unfortunately, the expansion of CMHCs did not solve the problem of chronicity in mental illness. In fact, some argue that the centers exacerbated the plight of the chronic patient (Bassuk and Gerson 1978). In many communities, the CMHC extended services to new populations of previously untreated individuals, largely ignoring the populations traditionally served by state mental hospitals (Windle and Scully 1976). At the same time, the promise of the CMHCs, especially for reducing the resident census of state mental hospitals and saving resources, helped to promote a policy called "deinstitutionalization" (Bachrach 1976). This policy, together with the entitlement programs under the

Social Security Act, led to the discharge of hundreds of thousands of mental patients from psychiatric hospitals.[2] CMHCs were almost totally unprepared (or unwilling, or both) to shoulder the responsibility of this chronic population. They saw their mission and their promise in the prevention of chronicity, not in dealing with the failures of previous approaches to mental health care.

The problem for centers was compounded by two additional factors: First, the "seed money" concept of annually decreasing federal resources often meant that centers had to abandon poorer patients with a pattern of high service utilization (such as chronic patients) in favor of insured patients who might respond to brief interventions (Weiner et al. 1979). Second, the CMHC program was a federal-local grant mechanism which avoided state involvement. This attempt to circumvent the state mental health agency in order to avoid control of CMHCs by "institution-minded bureaucrats" also meant that the depopulation of state mental hospitals would proceed without coordination with the CMHCs (Bassuk and Gerson 1978; GAO 1977).

Reassessing Deinstitutionalization   By the mid-1970s, the policy of deinstitutionalization was being severely criticized. Despite the optimism stimulated by the movement to deinstitutionalize mental health services, it was apparent by the mid-1970s that community care of the chronically mentally ill had brought with it new patterns of exclusion, neglect, and abuse. The many tragedies of deinstitutionalization were reported in vivid detail in mass media descriptions of ex-hospital patients sleeping outdoors on heating grates and in doorways, living in squalid single-room occupancies, wandering the streets, and trying desperately to get back into institutions in which they could feel secure and safe. Journalistic accounts asked, "Where is my home?" (NIMH 1974) and decried the move "out of their beds and into the streets" (AFSCME 1975) and from "back wards to back alleys" (Trotter and Kuttner 1974). Some observers felt that conditions in the communities were as bad as those in the institutions which proponents of deinstitutionalization were trying to replace. Others thought that current policies were recreating the same preasylum conditions that led to the reformist efforts of Horace Mann and Dorothea Dix in the beginning of the nineteenth century.

CMHCs and the community mental health movement were taking a large share of the blame for their unresponsiveness to a problem they did not create (GAO 1977). Like the asylum and psychopathic hospitals before them, centers did fail to meet the idealized expectations of the reformers who introduced them. In each case, it was the difficulty of curing the chronic patient that led to disillusionment.

A NETWORK OF CARING

Out of the failure of the community mental health movement to address adequately the needs of the chronically mentally ill came the CSP, NIMH's "pilot approach." Although the 1977 General Accounting Office Report, *Returning the Mentally Disabled to the Community: Government Needs to Do More,* gave the CSP its most significant push forward, the program actually developed out of an NIMH work group begun in 1974.

A "Community Support Work Group" was formed by Lucy Ozarin within the Division of Mental Health Service Programs at NIMH to promote and develop a community-based system of care for "mentally handicapped adults."[3] Supported by NIMH director, Bertram Brown, and Service Program Division director, Frank Ochberg, this work group expanded its membership to include representatives from all NIMH divisions and other interested federal agencies. The work group became a task force "to update the NIMH Hospital Improvement Program and the Hospital Staff Development Program." Under the staff leadership of Judith Turner, William TenHoor, and G. Bart Stone, the work group and task force recommended a CSP to be developed out of a reallocation of existing resources previously used for state mental hospitals. In 1977, Director Brown authorized the development of CSP and appointed the new Acting Director of the Services Division, Steven S. Sharfstein, chairman of a CSP implementation group. Later that same year, the first requests for proposals were solicited.

Three conclusions underlie the decision to develop a new categorical program. First, it was clear to all responsible observers that the needs of people with chronic mental illness extended well beyond the boundaries of the mental health system. In order to meet the comprehensive needs of this population, it would be necessary to coordinate efforts with a broad array of health and social welfare agencies. Second, even within the mental health system, it was necessary to promote the development of local agencies willing and able to make long-term commitments to chronic patients who needed some services that were not easily reimbursable by third-party insurers. A third general conclusion was that there was a pervasive need to better clarify lines of responsibility for the chronic patients at all levels of government. As Turner and TenHoor (1978:323) state, "perhaps the most critical factor contributing to inadequacies in community-based care is fragmentation and confusion of responsibility among the many federal, state, and local agencies whose programs have an impact on services to the mentally disabled in the community." Accordingly, it was decided that NIMH should assume a leading role at the federal level, and that focal points of responsibility needed to be created at the state and local levels.

Community Support Systems   A major thrust of the CSP was to promote the concept of the CSS, defined by NIMH (1977:1, appendix A) as "a network of caring and responsible people committed to assisting a vulnerable population to meet their needs and develop their potential without being unnecessarily isolated or excluded from the community." The vulnerable population in question consisted of "adult psychiatric patients whose disabilities are severe and persistent but for whom long-term skilled or semiskilled nursing care is inappropriate" (Turner and TenHoor 1978:319).[4] This noninstitutionalized segment of the chronically mentally ill is estimated to number between 800,000 and 1.5 million persons (Goldman, Gattozzi, and Taube 1981).

The CSS concept paralleled the "balanced service system" (Melville 1977) and a variety of psychosocial rehabilitation models, broadening the approach to the treatment of the chronically mentally ill. The concept is based on theories and research indicating the critical role of social support networks (i.e. family members, relatives, friends, coworkers) in the adjustment of the mentally ill in the community. (Brown and Harris 1978; Cobb 1976; Dean and Lin 1977; Henderson 1980; Mechanic 1979a; 1979b, Miller and Ingham 1976; Mueller 1980; Turner 1981). This extensive literature suggests that natural support systems could be reinforced by a comprehensive network of services.

A comprehensive support system provides for case identification, outreach services, assistance in applying for entitlements, crisis-stabilization services in the least restrictive setting, an array of psychosocial rehabilitation services, sheltered living arrangements, medical and mental health care, and backup support to families and friends. Other essential components of a CSS include involving concerned community members in providing services and opportunities, protecting client rights, and providing case management (Turner and TenHoor 1978).

The CSP planners were quick to realize that even in the community it is necessary to fulfill many of the basic human needs that were previously met by the mental hospital. These needs include those related to food, clothing, shelter, recreation, religion, medical and mental health care, social services for families, legal services, transportation, and communication. Many of these tasks are immensely more complicated when clients are dispersed in the community (rather than in a "total institution") and responsibilities for their care are fragmented. In addition, some CSP services are new and arise out of the decentralization of the mental health system. One such service is case management. Transportation is also more important in a decentralized system than it was in the total institution, and shelter has been reorganized in the community as a continuum arrayed in terms of such dimensions as restrictiveness, size, and intensity of professional supervision.

The name "Community Support System" is also telling, in so far as it suggests the CSP planners' commitment to compensate for the dearth of natural support systems available to most chronic mental patients. Unfortunately, persons with long-term and disabling mental disorders are often handicapped in their abilities to build and sustain social support networks. As others have observed, the experience of such persons in feeling needed and useful to others is often quite limited, and some patients have no one person in their lives who consistently cares about their welfare (Turner and Shifren 1979).

By 1978, nineteen states had been awarded CSP contracts "amounting to a total of approximately $3.5 million for the first year's activities" (Turner and TenHoor 1978:319). These contracts involved the transfer of funds from NIMH to state mental health agencies, many of which also subcontracted with local community programs. Contracts were awarded to states and programs that had already established a capacity for innovation. The CSP contracts were designed to develop statewide strategies for implementing CSSs and to encourage model program development. As Turner and TenHoor (1978:340) explain, "the CSP attempts to use a very small amount of Federal money to stimulate the development of a full array of such programs within the context of a planned accountable system." The fact that contract funds went directly to state mental health authorities reversed the trend established by the CMHCs Program. States controlled the resources, but NIMH specified ten essential components and four conditions necessary for constituting a system (See Table 1–2). These guidelines went far beyond the CMHC concept of mental health services.

The program received further support from the President's Commission on Mental Health (1978) and from the NP/CMI (1981). In 1980, The CSP became a permanent organizational component of NIMH as the Community Support and Rehabilitation Branch. NIMH awarded contracts for three years until CSP was converted to a grant program. This change was prompted, in part, by the passage of the Mental Health Systems Act (MHSA). However, in 1981, before the act could be implemented, the first categorical grants were awarded.

ASSESSING THE CSP

CSP has offered great promise. But, is it working? Is the CSP and its concept of a CSS a real solution to the problem of the chronic patient? Can the models developed be generalized? (Bachrach 1980). Does CSP represent a fundamental reform or a minor modification, a mid-course correction, in the community mental health movement and for CMHCs? Will the result be a brief attempt at the revival of reform during the decline of community-based care, like Bemis' failed attempt to restore moral treatment, or will reform interests prevail? Will the reform be undermined by competing professional interests and fiscal conservatism? Does it represent a final gasp before a backlash return to large scale institutionalization, or will the CSP model persist at the state

Table 1–2.   Components of a Community Support System.

CSP guidelines specify that however a particular state or community arranges its services, an adequate system for the severely mentally disabled must fix responsibility and provide staff and resources to perform the following functions:[4]

1. Identification of the target population, whether in hospitals or in the community, and outreach to offer appropriate services to those willing to participate
2. Assistance in applying for entitlements
3. Crisis stabilization services in the least restrictive setting possible, with hospitalization available when other options are insufficient
4. Psychosocial rehabilitation services, including but not limited to:
   • goal-oriented rehabilitation evaluation
   • training in community living skills, in the natural setting wherever possible
   • opportunities to improve employability
   • appropriate living arrangements in an atmosphere that encourages improvements in functioning
   • opportunities to develop social skills, interests, and leisure-time activities to provide a sense of participation and worth.
5. Supportive services of indefinite duration, including supportive living and working arrangements, and other such services for as long as they are needed
6. Medical and mental health care
7. Backup support to families, friends, and community members
8. Involvement of concerned community members in planning and offering housing or working opportunities
9. Protection of client rights, both in hospitals and in the community
10. Case management, to ensure continuous availability of appropriate forms of assistance

Conditions Necessary for Constituting a System

Assuming that all of the above opportunities and services are available within a given planning area, the following conditions

Table 1–2.   continued

---

are considered prerequisites for constituting a system (CSP RFPs 1977):
1. The comprehensive needs of the population at risk must be assessed
2. There must be legislative, administrative, and financial arrangements to guarantee that appropriate forms of assistance are available to meet these needs
3. There must be a core services agency within the community that is committed to helping severely mentally disabled people improve their lives
4. There must be an individual person (or team) at the client level responsible for remaining in touch with the client on a continuing basis, regardless of how many agencies get involved

---

and local levels, despite the cutbacks in federal money and influence?

The purpose of this book is to provide further national visibility to the CSP model, and to bring together and synthesize data based on the NIMH experience. Like the program it seeks to assess, CSP evaluation is in its infancy. Some evaluation goals have been accomplished, but much work remains. This book describes the recent NIMH accomplishments, as well as an agenda of unfinished business and some directions for the future. As subsequent chapters will detail, a good deal of conceptual work was done to determine information needs and evaluation objectives. On this basis, an evaluation strategy was developed. Methodologies were pilot tested, and some substantive knowledge was gleaned concerning the implementation of CSP at the state level, the size and characteristics of the target population, clients' use of available services, and factors affecting adjustment to community living. But, in terms of our total agenda for evaluation, what we have yet to learn is certainly greater than what we know definitively.

Significance   The significance of this book lies both in its practical value and in its relevance to the field of mental health policy.

From a practical standpoint, what we learned about CSPs can be used to influence state mental health authorities to mount their own programs for the chronically mentally ill. While categorical funds for CSPs may no longer be available, all fifty states will receive block grants for alcohol, drug abuse, and mental health programs. Some portion of these block grants can be used to support a comprehensive approach to meeting the needs of the chronically mentally ill.

Also, from a practical standpoint, our methods for learning about CSPs may stimulate and help guide evaluation activities for those CSPs which receive support through the block grant or through other state revenues. As Schulberg and Bromet (1981:930) note, the continuance and expansion of CSSs

> must be justified in terms of the benefits that they produce. Administrators and legislators overwhelmed with competing claims on limited public funds will soon seek outcome data pertaining to the services' value. Although fiscal appropriations ultimately may be determined by political or other criteria, data about effectiveness are nevertheless vital to the mental health planner's case for continued or expanded funding.

In terms of mental health policy, the case of CSP brings into focus the many ways in which the larger societal context raises barriers to the diffusion and implementation of CSPs on a broad national scale. David Mechanic (1979b:10) has recently addressed this issue in terms of the distinction between innovation and follow through:

> In the mental health arena the problem has not been lack of motivation, but rather a lack of organizational follow through. It has been difficult to encourage serious evaluation of varying innovations, and, thus, to distinguish between those that are truly effective as compared with those that are simply fads. Once particular approaches have been found to be superior to conventional services, it has been difficult to achieve their widespread adoption because of reimbursement rules, and the pattern of traditionally organized professional agencies and relations. Innovation requires more than having a good idea. It necessitates understanding financial aspects of care, political organization of services and interprofessional relationships.

Related observations about the limitations of model programs have been made by Leona Bachrach who has emphasized the idiosyncratic nature of model programs, their lack of comparability, and the many questions surrounding their generalizability (Bachrach 1980). In the Carter administration, the NIMH CSP generated much excitement, drew talented people to work on its behalf, and accepted evaluation as an integral part of the program. Though the strong federal role is about to be eclipsed, all of the problems facing the chronically mentally ill remain, and any future initiative designed to enhance the quality of life of the chronic mental patient, whether on the federal, state, or local level, will have to come to grips with the generic issues and dilemmas discussed in this book. In this sense, the book is only, in part, a retrospective analysis of the latest cycle of reform in mental health policy toward the chronically mentally ill. It is also prospective, providing a window into the future and a critical look at the challenge of caring for persons with chronic mental disorders in community rather than institutional settings.

NOTES

1. In order to put the political events that followed the election of 1980 into proper perspective, it is important to note that some states already had embraced the concept of a CSS prior to the advent of CSP at the federal level in 1977, and that service configurations similar to the CSP model existed in numerous communities throughout the United States. For example, the New York State budget for CSSs is actually larger than the entire NIMH budget, and New York's commitment to a community support model antedates the NIMH initiative. Similar observations can be made about Massachusetts, Colorado, New Jersey, and several other states. It may be inferred that the fate of the CSP model does not depend solely on federal support.

2. Attempts to understand this complex process are detailed in the literature (see, for example, Gruenberg and Archer 1979; Klerman 1977; Kramer 1977).

3. Turner and TenHoor (1978) outlined the development of the CSP from this work group to a task force and ultimately to a NIMH program.

4. We use 1977 guidelines at this point in the text to be historically correct. In future chapters we use more current CSP guidelines as a point of reference.

REFERENCES

American Federation of State, County, and Municipal Employees. 1975. *Deinstitutionalization: Out of Their Beds and into the Streets.* Washington, D.C.: A.F.S.C.M.E. (February).

Bachrach, L. L. 1976. *Deinstitutionalization: An Analytic Review and Sociological Perspective.* DHEW Publication No. (ADM) 76–351. Washington, D.C.: Government Printing Office.

———. 1980. "Model Programs for Chronic Mental Patients." *American Journal of Psychiatry* 137, 1023–31.

Bassuk, E. L., and J. Gerson. 1978. "Deinstitutionalization and Mental Health Services." *Scientific American* 238: 46–53.

Beers, C. 1908. *A Mind That Found Itself.* New York: Longmans, Green.

Bockoven, J. S. 1972. *Moral Treatment in Community Mental Health.* New York: Springer.

Brown, G. W., and T. Harris. 1978. *Social Origins of Depression.* New York: The Free Press.

Caplan. R. B. 1969. *Psychiatry and the Community in Nineteenth Century America.* New York: Basic Books.

Cobb, S. 1976. "Social Support as a Moderator of Life Stress." *Psychosomatic Medicine* 38: 301–14.

Dain, N. 1980. "The Chronic Mental Patient in 19th-Century America." *Psychiatric Annals* 10, no. 9(September): 323–27.

Dean, A., and N. Lin. 1977. "The Stress Buffering Role of Social Support." *Journal of Nervous and Mental Disease* 165: 403–17.

Deutsch, A. 1948. *The Shame of the States.* New York: Harcourt, Brace.

General Accounting Office. 1977. *Returning the Mentally Disabled to the Community: Government Needs to Do More.* Washington, D.C.: General Accounting Office.

Goldman, H.H.; A. A. Gattozzi; and C.A. Taube. 1981. "Defining and Counting the Chronically Mentally Ill." *Hospital and Community Psychiatry* 32, no. 1 (January): 21–27.

Grob, G.N. 1966. *The State and the Mentally Ill: A History of Worcester State Hospital in Massachusetts, 1830–1920.* Chapel Hill: University of North Carolina Press.

———. 1973. *Mental Institutions in America: Social Policy to 1875.* New York: The Free Press.

Gruenberg, E. and J. Archer. 1979. "Abandonment of Responsibility for the Seriously Mentally Ill." *Milbank Memorial Fund Quarterly/ Health and Society* 57: 485-506.

Henderson, S. 1980. "A Development in Social Psychiatry: The Systematic Study of Social Bonds." *Journal of Nervous and Mental Disease* 168: 63–69.

Joint Commission on Mental Illness and Health. 1961. *Action for Mental Health.* New York: Basic Books.

Klerman, G. L. 1977. "Better But Not Well: Social and Ethical Issues in the Deinstitutionalization of the Mentally Ill." *Schizophrenia Bulletin* 3, no. 4: 617-631.

Kramer, M. 1977. "Psychiatric Services and the Changing Institutional Scene, 1950-1985." DHEW Publication No. (ADM) 77-433. Washington, D.C.: U.S. Government Printing Office.

Levinson, A. I., and B.S. Brown. 1967. "Some Implications of the Community Mental Health Center Concept." In *Social Psychiatry,* edited by P. Hoch and J. Zubin. New York: Grune & Stratton.

Linn, L. 1961. *Frontiers in General Hospital Psychiatry.* New York: International University Press.

Mechanic, D. 1979a. "Community Integration of the Mentally Ill." In *Future Issues in Health Care.* pp. 64–74. New York: The Free Press.

———. 1979b. "Community Support of the Chronically Mentally Ill." Keynote Address, National Institute of Mental Health Learning Community Conference, Washington, D.C.

Melville, C. 1977. *The Balanced Service System.* Contract report to the Joint Commission on Accreditation of Hospitals. Atlanta, Georgia: Georgia Mental Health Institute. Mimeo.

Milbank Memorial Fund. 1962. *Decentralization of Psychiatric Services and Continuity of Care.* New York: Milbank Memorial Fund.

Miller, P., and J. Ingham. 1976. "Friends, Confidants and Symptoms." *Social Psychiatry* 11:51.

Mora, G. 1967. "The History of Psychiatry." In *Comprehensive Textbook of Psychiatry,* edited by A. Freedman and H. Kaplan, pp. 1–34. Baltimore: Williams and Williams.

Morrissey, J. P.; H.H. Goldman; L.V. Klerman and Associates. 1980. *The Enduring Asylum.* New York: Grune & Stratton.

Mueller, D.P. 1980. "Social Networks: A Promising Direction for Research on the Relationship of the Social Environment to Psychiatric Disorder." *Social Science and Medicine* 14A: 147–61.

National Institute of Mental Health. 1974. "Where Is My Home?" Proceedings of a Conference on the Closing of State Mental Hospitals, Scottsdale, Arizona, February 14–15. Stanford Research Institute (May).

National Institute of Mental Health—Community Support Selection. 1977. "Request for Proposals No. NIMH-MH-77-0080-0081." (July). Mimeo.

"National Plan for the Chronically Mentally Ill." 1980. Final Draft Report to the Secretary of Health and Human Services, Washington, D.C.: D.H.H.S. (August).

President's Commission on Mental Health. 1978. Final Report. Washington, D.C.: Superintendent of Documents, U.S. Government Printing Office.

Rothman, D.J. 1980. *Conscience and Convenience: The Asylum and Its Alternatives in Progressive America.* Boston: Little Brown and Co.

———. 1971. *The Discovery of the Asylum.* Boston: Little Brown and Co.

Schulberg, H.C., and E. Bromet. 1981. "Strategies for Evaluating the Outcome of Community Services for the Chronically Mentally Ill." *American Journal of Psychiatry* 138, no. 7: 930–35.

Trotter S., and B. Kuttner. 1974. "Back Wards to Back Alleys." *Washington Post* (February 24).

Turner, R.J. 1981. "Social Support as a Contingency in Psychological Well-Being." *Journal of Health and Social Behavior* 22 (December): 357–67.

Turner, J.C., and I. Shifren. 1979. "Community Support Systems: How Comprehensive?" *New Directions for Mental Health Services* 2:1–13.

Turner, J.C., and W.J. TenHoor. 1978. "The NIMH Community Support Program: Pilot Approach to a Needed Social Reform." *Schizophrenia Bulletin* 4: 319–48.

Weiner, R.S.; J.R. Woy; S.S. Sharfstein; and R.D. Bass. 1979. "Community Mental Health Centers and the 'Seed Money' Concept: Effects of Terminating Federal Funds." *Community Mental Health Journal* 15, no. 2 (Summer): 129–39.

Windle, C., and D. Scully. 1976. "Community Mental Health Centers and the Decreasing Use of State Mental Hospitals." *Community Mental Health Journal* 12: 239–43.

2 APPROACH AND SOURCES OF DATA

The need to evaluate the Community Support Program (CSP) was apparent from its very beginning. With the first award of contracts for state strategy development and local demonstrations in 1977, program management encouraged evaluation. Turner and TenHoor (1978) describe a research ethos which surrounded the creation of the national CSP and supported the idea that the state and local projects were experimental models to be studied by the National Institute of Mental Health (NIMH). Certainly the projects presented a unique opportunity to collect data on the program and on the clients it served. The CSP contracts themselves indicated the value placed on evaluation. Evaluation was included as a task in all first-year contracts and contracting states were required to cooperate in a national evaluation of the program.

Prospects for evaluation activity were fostered by the availability of a special pool of funds. Law requires that one percent of the federal human services budget be set aside each year to evaluate government programs (called "1% evaluation"). As an innovative program, CSP was a good candidate for evaluation: Program management was receptive, data were obtainable from contract sites, and NIMH was able to recruit staff to work on the evaluation. We (Richard Tessler and Howard Goldman) were among those recruited.

Although the opportunity was enticing, the difficulties in designing and implementing appropriate studies were formidable. From an evaluation perspective, it was a mixed blessing that the program was relatively new and still in a pilot stage. While evaluation may take on a more important role in a pilot program which is still flexible and open to change, some anxiety about negative findings is inevitable, and evaluators also feel pressure to produce data quickly so that continued or expanded funding for the program can be justified. One dilemma the evaluation team faced was how to gather, analyze, and report data in a timely fashion without jeopardizing the scientific integrity of the studies. Good science is deliberate and exacting and, as such, difficult to integrate with administrative and budgetary timetables. Inertia was also introduced by the bureaucratic environment in which these studies were conceived. In the federal government, the review process for evaluation contracts is extremely cumbersome, especially when data are to be collected in a systematic fashion from more than nine entities and when respondent burden and confidentiality are matters of concern. In such cases, formal approval by the Office of Managment and the Budget (OMB) is required before data collection may commence.

The evaluation team also faced some state-of-the-art problems. First, there existed few, if any, precedents for CSP evaluation. The programmatic intervention was ambitious, innovative, and complex, with many different supporting activities attempting to improve the system of care at the federal, state, and local levels, and ultimately the quality of life of individual clients. Given the scope of the program, and considering that resources for evaluation were limited in terms of money, time, and staff, it was not at all clear where evaluation should begin and how priorities should be established. The state of the art was limited at all levels of analysis—perhaps most so at the systems level where instrumentation appropriate for the measurement of system change was simply not available. As we shall see in Chapter 9, the assessment of system change continues to be a major challenge in CSP evaluation. It was also unclear how best to proceed with the collection of data at the client level. What should be the sources of data about clients, and how could the reliability and validity of the data be assured?

Another difficulty involved the relationship between the evaluation staff and the program. Evaluation activity was initiated by specialists on the staff of the CSP, but subsequently, responsibility for evaluation of the program was transferred to another division at NIMH—the Division of Biometry and Epidemiology (DBE). This division already had assumed considerable responsibility for the collection of data used in the evaluation of the Community Mental Health Center (CMHC) Program.

Underlying this transfer of responsibility within NIMH were a number of difficult issues: Who should conduct the evaluation? Can "insiders" (that is, CSP staff) be objective about their own program, and would their conclusions be credible? Can "outsiders" be sensitive to the many nuances of the program, and would their studies be nontrivial and the results programmatically useful? Throughout the evaluation of CSP, the evaluation staff operated on the assumption that good evaluation required distance from, as well as familiarity with, the program. Accordingly, we met frequently with program staff and on many occasions invited their input, but as members of the DBE, the evaluation team also preserved some autonomy. In this manner, we attempted to function both as sympathetic insiders and as skeptical outsiders.

Just as important as the relationship between the evaluation and program staffs at NIMH were the relationships between the NIMH evaluators and the project staff at the state and local levels. Cooperation with state and local contractors was vital if we were to secure appropriate data. Cooperation was threatened, however, by at least two factors. First, data collection is burdensome to state and local administrators and to case managers faced with many needy clients. Individuals responsible for delivering community support services must be persuaded of the importance of evaluation, and methods that minimize the burden thereby imposed must be fashioned. Second, state and local agenda for evaluation are not always compatible with federal needs for uniform data. Where the two agenda conflict (as they sometimes did), resistance frequently develops. In order for national evaluation to succeed, a working partnership must be created between the federal government and its state and local contractors.

Out of this mix of opportunity and challenge evolved a more or less coherent approach to evaluation. The purpose of the remainder of this chapter is to explain this strategy in terms of its origin and underlying rationale, to describe the implementation process and the different studies that were conducted, and finally, to analyze some problems and issues that emerged during the conduct of these studies.

THE EVALUATION STRATEGY

In the federal government, evaluation strategies tend to evolve as evaluation and program staff seek to reconcile scientific standards, political pressures, and bureaucratic constraints. Such was the case with CSP evaluation.

Program management initiated a discussion of a strategy for CSP evaluation by taking the following concrete steps: (1) Herbert Schulberg was commissioned to prepare a concept paper on CSP evaluation; (2) NIMH staff developed a series of questions considered pertinent to the national evaluation; and (3) evaluation workshops were convened at three "Learning Community Conferences" sponsored by NIMH.[1] In addition, a special evaluation conference was held in March 1978. In this manner, CSP management sought to set in motion a participatory process that would result in shared understanding about evaluation needs and priorities.

Discussion of evaluation options for CSP was enriched by consulation with national experts in the evaluation of human service programs. Schulberg, a professor of clinical psychiatry and psychology at the University of Pittsburg School of Medicine, delivered his concept paper entitled "Strategies for Evaluating the Outcome of Community Support Programs" at the Third Learning Community Conference (Schulberg 1978). Outcomes were conceived in terms of CSP's potential impact on clients, families, staff, and communities.[2] In a related paper entitled "Community Support Programs: Program Evaluation and Public Policy," Schulberg proposed a multifaceted approach to CSP evaluation which would include assessment of the population-at-risk, the population served, availability and cost, strategies for systems change, and CSP benefits for clients (Schulberg 1979).

The evolution of a strategy for CSP evaluation was further influenced by consultation with Amitai Etzioni of the Brookings

Institution. Etzioni advocated a step-by-step approach to evaluation based on a recognition that CSP was in a formative stage. He cautioned against the danger of "premature evaluation" and urged that descriptive, methodological, and exploratory studies were most appropriate at this time.

Underlying any evaluation strategy is a set of assumptions that provide direction and focus to evaluation activities. In the case of CSP evaluation, three basic assumptions emerged out of the participatory and consultation processes described above. The consensus that evolved around these assumptions helps to account for many of the choices that were subsequently made and the kinds of data that were ultimately collected.

One basic assumption was that CSP should be evaluated in relation to its own goals and objectives, and in conjunction with operationally defined and agreed-upon measures of program performance. The individuals who participated in the planning of actual studies were concerned that the evaluation of the program be fair, and that the results be relevant to CSP management and potentially useful for program planning and policy-making. Accordingly, it made sense to begin where the program was rather than to impose an external set of criteria for evaluation. It was also agreed that CSP evaluation should be restricted to objectives for which the program could be realistically held accountable. In this manner, analysis of CSP's logical structure and measurement potential was to serve as a central component in the overall evaluation strategy.

A second assumption underlying the evaluation strategy was that client-level data were important. Without knowledge of who CSP clients were and how they utilized available services, management would be unable to determine if the program was reaching those clients for whom it was designed, and whether they were being comprehensively served. By the same token, it seemed important to estimate the number and characteristics of chronically mentally ill persons in the target population in order to assess the need for community support systems (CSSs) in the United States and to plan for the future.

Assessment of client outcome was a somewhat different matter. Whether clients benefit from CSP is, of course, the ultimate evaluation question. But, for two reasons, systematic study of the "client benefit" hypothesis was regarded as premature. First, the design and implementation of such studies went beyond the present state of the art. We had no prior experience collecting uniform data on CSP clients from case managers, and we also lacked demonstrably reliable and valid measures for such key client-outcome variables as quality of life. "Benefit" and "quality of life" are so subjective that operationalization is difficult. Second, client outcome studies were also regarded as premature because of the status of CSP as a pilot program, still in a formative stage. Only some of CSP's limited resources were being used for direct services to clients. Most resources were being concentrated on a system change strategy, and time was necessary for reforms to show their intended effects. For these reasons, studies of client outcome were deferred to when the program would be better established and when some of the state-of-the-art problems had been addressed by exploratory and methodological studies.

A third assumption underlying the evaluation strategy was that it was important to assess CSP's impact on the service delivery system. Although client outcome is an important measure of program success, it is not the only level upon which a program can be assessed. Evaluation studies can also assess whether a program is having an impact by virtue of its success in increasing awareness of the needs of the target population and changing the system of care to be more responsive to these needs (Department of Health and Human Services 1980). As Chapter 3 will show, system change objectives are basic to the intent and logic of CSP.

In summary, the evaluation strategy for CSP assigned highest priority to program analysis, descriptions of clients in local demonstrations as well as others in need of CSSs, and the assessment of system change. Evaluation planners reasoned that a step-by-step approach was most appropriate, and chose to defer some research issues for future consideration.

IMPLEMENTATION

As used in the present section, implementation refers to those activities that intervene between conceptualizing an evaluation strategy and actually signing contracts for data collection and analysis. Implementing a national evaluation strategy can be exceedingly complex and time consuming. It is nonetheless a critical step in the evaluation process; many a well-conceived evaluation strategy has gone awry when confronted with the bureaucratic problems involved. In the present section we describe the more salient bureaucratic events and identify some of the individuals who played significant roles in translating shared assumptions about CSP evaluation into government contracts.[3]

At the Learning Community Conferences, evaluators agreed upon the need for a uniform client data instrument (UCDI) to describe the CSP client on a national basis. Such data would enable CSP to describe the people it was serving and their use of services, and allow for comparisons between clients at different demonstration sites. Case managers would be expected to provide data on their clients involved in the study. With these goals in mind, evaluators from state mental health offices in New York, Colorado, and Michigan collaborated with NIMH in the development of a UCDI.[4] Ultimately the instrument was divided into three distinct sections covering background information, clinical history and current social functioning, and utilization of services.

As evaluation activities expanded, the need for an individual or group to coordinate these efforts became apparent. This need was met for a time by Nancy Wilson, a program evaluator from the Department of Mental Health in Colorado who worked in CSP between 1978 and 1979 on an Intergovernmental Personnel Assignment (I.P.A.). In collaboration with Jerry Storck of CSP and Beatrice Rosen and Howard Goldman, both of the DBE, Wilson conceived and drafted supporting documentation for a field test of the UCDI and for an analysis of CSP needs-assessment data. The latter study, to be described in more detail later in this chapter, was to focus on the size, characteristics, and needs of chronically mentally ill persons constituting CSP's target population.

The expiration of Wilson's I.P.A., and her return to Colorado, created a serious vacuum in CSP evaluation at the federal level. As an interim step, Howard Goldman was asked to increase his time consulting CSP on evaluation issues. In the spring of 1979 responsiblity for CSP evaluation was formally transferred to the DBE. Concurrently, Richard Tessler was recruited by DBE to work full time on the CSP evaluation. Tessler and DBE "inherited" Wilson's two projects and Beatrice Rosen, then head of the Needs Assessment and Evaluation Section within DBE, agreed to serve as government project officer once these contracts were let.

In the summer of 1979, a CSP evaluation policy board was convened, consisting of NIMH staff from DBE and the Division of Mental Health Service Programs.[5] This policy board delineated specific evaluation activities for the coming fiscal year, and through regular meetings sought to assure timely communication between program and evaluation staff.

Two other events helped to set the stage for evaluation activities in the year ahead. One was the 1980 "1% Evaluation Plan" for NIMH-sponsored mental health services which highlighted CSP evaluation as a NIMH priority. The other occurred in September 1979 when the Office of the Assistant Secretary for Planning and Evaluation (ASPE) approached NIMH through the latter's Office of Program Development and Analysis (OPDA) in search of one or more programs interested in an "Evaluability Assessment (EA).[6] The prospect of an EA of CSP was exciting to those of us who were planning CSP evaluation, because we believed that it would provide an excellent opportunity for in-depth analysis of the program's logic and performance. This type of evaluation was fully compatible with the importance assigned to program analysis as part of a comprehensive evaluation strategy. Because of a preexisting arrangement between ASPE and a contractor (Macro Systems, Inc.), it was possible to convene the EA in relatively short order.

Hence, in October 1979, the start of the new fiscal year in government, the CSP evaluation strategy was translated into specific studies. In the following section we present some descriptive material about the studies themselves, but first we describe the contracting process which set these studies in motion.

THE 1% EVALUATION CONTRACTS

Due to federal staff shortages, the government usually contracts with private consulting firms for assistance in conducting its 1 percent evaluation studies. The contractual process at NIMH is illustrated in Figure 2–1.

This flow chart shows the events that are required to occur prior to the award of a government contract. In brief, these events consist of the development of a request for proposals (RFP), the publication of a notice in the Commerce Business Dai-

Figure 2–1.   Federal Evaluation Activities.

```
                          ┌─────────────┐
                          │ Parameters of│◄───────────────────────┐
                          │ Activity Are │                         │
                          │ Delineated  │                         │
                          └─────────────┘                         │
              ┌──────────────────┴───────────────────┐           │
              ▼                                       ▼           │
    ┌──────────────────┐                   ┌──────────────────┐  │
    │ Evaluation Policy│                   │   Requests for   │  │
    │    Board Is      │                   │   Proposal Are   │  │
    │    Convened      │                   │    Developed     │  │
    └──────────────────┘                   └──────────────────┘  │
              │                                       ▲           │
              ▼                                       │           │
    ┌──────────────────┐                   ┌──────────────────┐  │
    │  CSP Evaluation  │                   │   Notices Are    │  │
    │  Activities Are  │         Yes       │  Published in    │  │
    │   Delineated     │                   │    Commerce      │  │
    └──────────────────┘                   │ Business Daily   │  │
              │                             └──────────────────┘  │
              ▼                                       │           │
         ◆──────────◆                       ┌──────────────────┐  │
        ╱    Do     ╲──────────────────────►│ Technical Review │  │
       ◆ Activities Involve                 │   Committees     │  │
        ╲ Contracting?╱                      │  Are Convened    │  │
         ◆──────────◆                       └──────────────────┘  │
              │ No                                    │           │
              ▼                             ┌──────────────────┐  │
    ┌──────────────────┐                   │    Technical     │  │
    │  Activities Are  │                   │  Proposals Are   │  │
    │   Implemented    │                   │    Evaluated     │  │
    └──────────────────┘                   └──────────────────┘  │
              │                                       │           │
              ▼                             ┌──────────────────┐  │
    ┌──────────────────┐                   │ Technical Review │  │
    │    Evaluate      │                   │    Summary       │  │
    │    Federal       │                   └──────────────────┘  │
    │   Evaluation     │                             │           │
    │   Activities     │                   ┌──────────────────┐  │
    └──────────────────┘                   │  Contracts Are   │  │
              │                             │    Awarded       │  │
              │                             └──────────────────┘  │
              │                                       │           │
              │                             ┌──────────────────┐  │
              │                             │   Implement      │  │
              │                             │   Contracts      │  │
              │                             └──────────────────┘  │
              │                                       │           │
              │                             ┌──────────────────┐  │
              │                             │   Contract/      │  │
              │                             │   Contractor     │  │
              │                             │ Performance Is   │  │
              │                             │   Evaluated      │  │
              │                             └──────────────────┘  │
              │                                       │           │
              │                             ┌──────────────────┐  │
              └────────────────────────────►│   Evaluation    │──┘
                                            │  Information     │
                                            │  Is Compiled     │
                                            │    and Used      │
                                            └──────────────────┘
```

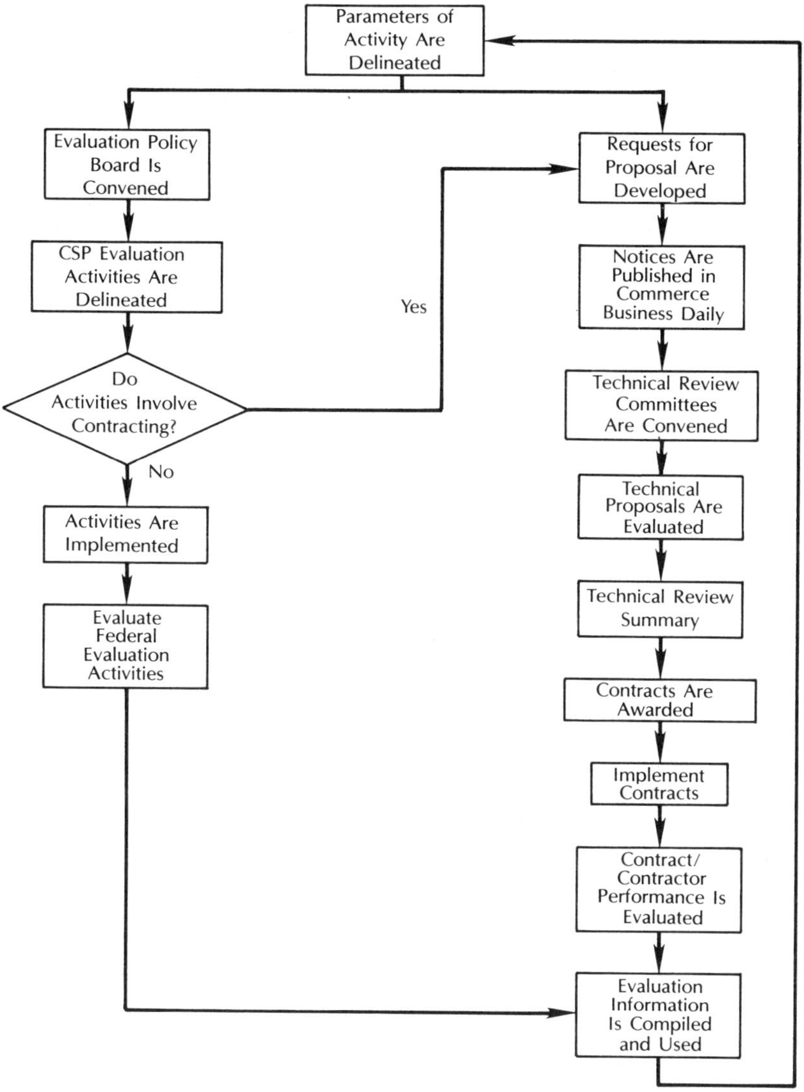

Source: Stroul, Morrison, Kotler, and Rienzo. (1980: Appendix C, 16).

ly, the convening of a technical review committee to evaluate submitted proposals, and the selection of a contractor based on considerations of quality as well as cost. When an evaluation contract requires data collection from more than nine respondents, as was the case in one of our studies, it is also necessary to obtain approval from the OMB.

Data from four evaluation contracts provide the basis for much of what follows in subsequent chapters. While further detail about each study is provided in these later chapters, it is instructive at this point to preview the studies through brief descriptions of their objectives and methodologies. We call these studies: The Evaluability Assessment, the Needs Assessment, the Client Survey, and the Short-Term Evaluation.

The *Evaluability Assessment* of the CSP, conducted under contract with Macro Systems, Inc., was undertaken by NIMH in collaboration with the Office of the ASPE. The objectives of the EA were: (1) to describe the logic of the CSP as it is viewed by program managers and policymakers; (2) to document actual program activities and functions at the state and local levels and to assess whether and to what extent the program, as implemented, conforms to federal intent; (3) to assess the plausibility and feasibility of the CSP's objectives and to identify realistic indicators of program performance; and (4) to formulate management and evaluation options for the future.

In accordance with these objectives, a work group consisting of persons from NIMH, ASPE, Office of the Assistant Secretary for Health, and Macro Systems, Inc. reviewed CSP documents and conducted interviews with program managers and others involved in policymaking at the national level. Members of the work group also went on field visits to a sample of state strategy development and local demonstration sites, and interviewed CSP personnel in regional offices. In addition, the work group met periodically with a federal policy group consisting of CSP managers, government evaluation specialists, and health policymakers. The EA results are presented in Chapters 3 and 4.

Another contract was for a *Needs-Assessment Study*. In entering into contractual agreements for state strategy development projects, each state was required to conduct a needs assessment in conjunction with its other first-year activities. However, guidelines were general and no specific approaches were dictated. Hence, a variety of disparate methods were used by states, ranging from simple approaches dealing only with clients already in community programs to broader population-based projections. To develop a more systematic and complete approach to the assessment of client needs, NIMH contracted with the Human Services Research Institute (HSRI) to evaluate the needs-assessment data already collected at the state level. A major objective was to identify and develop needs-assessment models suitable for future use at the state and national levels (Rosen and Tessler 1980). These models are summarized and discussed in Chapter 8.

In contrast to the needs-assessment study which focused on the characteristics and needs of the target population, *The Client Survey* was intended to describe the clients who were actually being served at local CSS demonstration sites. Under contract with Market Facts, Inc., the purpose of this project was to use the UCDI to gather information about CSP clients in three main areas: demographic information, clinical history and current social functioning, and services utilization. A brief section on the prevalence of client victimization, in terms of crimes against the client's person or property, was also included. A second purpose was to assess the feasibility of using case managers to report client-descriptive data.

The data were collected in the spring of 1980 from federally sponsored demonstration sites of CSP serving approximately forty-two hundred clients. Two hundred and forty-eight case managers completed forms for an average of seven clients each. In total, UCDIs were completed for 1,471 clients, making this one of the largest sources of current information about chronically mentally ill persons living in community settings. These data provide the basis for Chapters 6 and 7.

The other major CSP evaluation study focused on implementation at the state level; we refer to it as the *Short-Term Evaluation*. This study was conducted by Macro Systems, Inc., between October 1980 and April 1981 as a follow-up to the EA of the CSP. The purpose of the Short-Term Evaluation was to refine and, where necessary, develop measures of program performance and to pilot test these measures in nine states. Based on site visits to these state CSP offices, the data provide a preliminary description of CSP implementation at the state level during the first three years of program funding. The findings are presented in Chapter 5.

The four studies reviewed above reflect an early phase in federal efforts to evaluate the CSP. The EA is intended to clarify and assess the design of the national program in terms of its plausibility and accountability. The Needs-Assessment project seeks to clarify the size and characteristics of the target population. The Client Survey is designed to describe the characteristics of clients being served, to establish whether and to what extent CSP clients are living independently and functioning effectively, and to enumerate the range and intensity of services that clients are receiving. Finally, the Short-Term Evaluation assesses, in an exploratory manner, the impact which CSP is having on the service delivery system at the state level.

While none of these studies is likely to yield definitive conclusions about the program, the studies will provide preliminary answers to such pertinent questions as: What is the logic of the program? How is it viewed by program staff in the field? What are the needs of the target population? Who are the people who are currently receiving services? Is the program serving the population for whom it was designed? Are available services responsive to the multifaceted needs of severely disabled adults living in community settings? To what extent have CSP states succeeded in gaining access to mainstream resources for the chronically mentally ill? These are some of the questions to be addressed in subsequent chapters.

ISSUES AND PROBLEMS

We conclude this methods chapter with an analysis of two issues and problems that emerged during the conduct of the evaluation studies described in the prior section: (1) the ambiguous relationship between federal and state-local evaluation activities, and (2) the need for state-local cooperation in the face of tensions in intergovernmental relations.

Throughout this chapter we have focused on federally initiated evaluation activities, and largely have ignored evaluation studies initiated by CSP contract recipients at the state and local levels. Since its first contract awards, the national CSP office has sought to stimulate evaluation activities at the state and local levels. Evaluation "tasks" were required of all funded CSP projects. State strategy development projects were required to conduct needs assessments on a statewide basis, and local demonstration projects were required to formulate and implement "local evaluation plans."[7] These evaluation tasks resulted in a variety of data collection activities, reported in many interim and yearly reports to the national CSP office. Staff shortages at NIMH made review and timely feedback difficult, and prompted a reconsideration of the purpose and role of evaluation at the state and local levels. How should such activities relate to the national evaluation program that was taking shape at NIMH?

The question of the role and purpose of state-local evaluation activities was to emerge frequently in meetings at NIMH between federal evaluation and program staff. It was a difficult question to resolve. On the one hand, we did not want to stifle evaluation activity at the state and local levels. But neither did we want to use scarce program resources to support an activity that appeared to be suffering from lack of direction and accountability. Over time, a compromise did emerge. In consultation with the evaluation advisory board, it was decided to provide program dollars for two "optional evaluations" to be awarded to states on a competitive and one-time-only basis; other evaluation activities at the state and local levels were to be more limited in scope and, if possible, focused on practical problems regularly encountered in program planning and monitoring.

In effect, the decision to support two optional evaluations was based on a recognition of the considerable expertise which exists at the state and local levels, and NIMH's desire to delegate some of the responsibility for evaluation. Accordingly, proposals were invited, reviewed by an NIMH technical review committee, and two contract awards were ultimately made. One was to the state of New York to convene two mini-conferences on approaches to designing a quality-of-life assessment tool appropriate for CSP clients, and to recommend questions and scales to NIMH for use in future research on the chronically mentally ill. The other award was to the state of Colorado for the development of a methodology appropriate to the assessment of the cost effectiveness of CSSs. It was hoped that each of these studies would provide a methodological foundation which could be incorporated by NIMH in future studies of national scope.[8]

A second problem that emerged was the difficulty NIMH encountered in gaining the cooperation of local demonstration sites for the Client Survey. This problem, which caught the NIMH evaluation staff by surprise, illustrates the critical importance of intergovernmental relationships to the successful evaluation of federally funded programs. A brief description of the genesis of this problem follows.

The Client Survey was first conceived in the early Learning Community and Evaluation Conferences as a collaborative project involving evaluators from the federal, state, and local levels. To a large degree, the strains that developed two to three years later stemmed from a conviction that NIMH had expropriated the project as its own, and had disenfranchised the state and local participants.

Such feelings were fueled by the long and unanticipated delay in implementing the Client Survey, due largely to the need for OMB clearance. The problems encountered in obtaining OMB clearance, and the ensuing delay in the project, were difficult for state and local evaluation staff to understand and appreciate.[9] In any case, it is clear that some state-local evaluators experienced a growing isolation from the project and, in the words of one central state figure, a lack of "participation and ownership." In brief, it appeared that considerable resentment had developed toward the current federal evaluation staff as well as the private consulting firm which had been contracted to carry out the study. At least some state staff felt that they should have been more involved in the design of the RFP for the Client Survey, and in the selection of the contractor. This was impossible because federal regulations required independent RFP development and peer review of all evaluation contract proposals. These regulations necessitated a degree of distance between evaluators and state-local project personnel which, unfortunately, was sometimes viewed as secretive. When this perception occurred, its effect was to further alienate state and local programs whose cooperation was vital to the success of the Client Survey.

Meanwhile, several of the CSP-funded projects had pushed ahead with their own plans to collect client-level data. Free of the impediments of the federal bureaucracy, one state had already succeeded in collecting longitudinal data at three points in time, in three local demonstration sites, before the federal government was able to put its first cross-sectional survey into the field! While this was the only instance in which longitudinal data had been collected, other states had also begun to collect client-level data with instruments similar, but not identical, to the UCDI.

Conflict between NIMH and state-local evaluators surfaced publicly at the 4th Learning Community Conference, which was held in Washington, D.C., in November 1979. At a meeting convened to brief project staff on the logistics of the survey and to introduce representatives of Market Facts, Inc. (the contractor), many complaints were heard. State and local staff complained that compliance would be incompatible with their own evaluation agenda and data collection instruments. Some questioned the need for uniform client data when secondary analysis of local data sets was possible. Some also complained about the reporting burden that cooperation in the national study would impose on case managers. And, finally, some voiced suspicions that the data might be used to make invidious comparisons between projects. At this time, the possibility of collecting uniform client data in all fifteen federally funded demonstration sites was very much in doubt.

During the next few months, much of the time and energy of the federal evaluation and program staffs was focused on this problem, and in the end the federal government prevailed. It did so through a mix of persuasion and pressure. Persuasive efforts focused on the rationale for and potential uses of uniform client data. Pressure focused on the contractual obligation on each of the state and local projects to provide data for a national evaluation of CSP. In the end, each of the fifteen local demonstration sites participated at some level in the Client Survey. The cooperation of all of the sites in the federal evaluation of the CSP have made this book possible.

NOTES

1.   The Conference Proceedings are available from the CSP, Division of Mental Health Service Programs, NIMH. Learning Community Conferences bring together national, state, and local staff for technical assistance and information sharing.
2.   A revision of this paper was subsequetly published in the American Journal of Psychiatry (Schulberg and Bromet 1981).
3.   We wish to acknowledge the key role played by J. Richard Woy, Acting Chief, Program Analysis and Evaluation Branch, OPDA, NIMH, throughout the formulation and implementation of the CSP evaluation strategy.

4. Donald Lund, Walter Furman, Anne Nelson (New York), Richard
    Vaughn, Gail Barton (Michigan), and Michael Kirby (Colorado)
    made significant contributions to the development of this instru-
    ment.
5. The members of the evaluation policy board were Judith Turner,
    Jerry Storck, Robert Lilly, Ronald Manderscheid, Beatrice Rosen,
    Howard Goldman, and Richard Tessler.
6. Two excellent resource materials relevant to EA as a general ap-
    proach in the evaluation of federal programs are now available: See
    Wholey 1979; and Schmidt, Scanlon, and Bell 1978. The terms
    Evaluability Assessment and Exploratory Evaluation are used in-
    terchangeably in this book (see Chapter 4).
7. It is noteworthy that these evaluation activities were supported by
    "program dollars," in contrast to the studies of national scope
    which were supported by 1 percent evaluation dollars.
8. New York State's work on quality of life was carried out in collabo-
    ration with representatives from Massachusetts, Oregon, and Colo-
    rado, and in consultation with outside experts. The product of their
    work, *Quality of Life: Evaluating the Community Support Program,*
    which includes an annotated bibliography of pertinent studies, is
    currently available from the New York State Office of Mental
    Health, Bureau of Community Support Programs (June, 1980). Col-
    orado's developmental work on a cost-effectiveness model applicable
    to CSSs was carried out under the direction of Dr. James Sorenson,
    a national expert in cost-accounting procedures for mental health
    service programs (Sorenson and Kucic 1981).
9. Clearance procedures prescribed by OMB require prior review and
    approval by clearance officers in the NIMH, the Alcohol, Drug, and
    Mental Health Administration (ADAMHA), and the United States
    Public Health Service (PHS). In addition, at the NIMH level, the
    research design and instrumentation for the Client Survey were re-
    viewed by an Extramural Technical Review Committee (ETRC).
    Each stage in the review process was time consuming and considera-
    ble documentation was required. In total, approximately two years
    intervened between the time this review process was first set in mo-
    tion and the receipt of OMB clearance for the survey.

REFERENCES

Department of Health and Human Services. 1980. "Research and Evaluation." In *Toward a National Plan for the Chronically Mentally Ill.*

DHHS Publication No. (ADM) 81–1077 (December): Part 2 99–116. Washington, D.C.: Government Printing Office.

New York State Office of Mental Health. 1981. *Quality of Life: Evaluating the Community Support Program. Albany, New York: Bureau of Community Support Systems. Mimeo.*

Rosen, B. M., and R. C. Tessler. 1980. "An Overview of the NIMH Program to Evaluate the Community Support Program for the Chronically Mentally Ill." Paper presented at the annual meeting of the American Public Health Association, Detroit, Michigan, October 20.

Schmidt, R.; J. W. Scanlon; and J. B. Bell. 1978. *Evaluability Assessment: Making Public Programs Work Better.* Washington, D.C.: The Urban Institute.

Schulberg, H. C. 1978. "Strategies for Evaluating the Outcome of Community Support Programs." Unpublished paper, University of Pittsburgh.

————. 1979. "Community Support Programs: Program Evaluation and Public Policy." *American Journal of Psychiatry* 136, no. 11 (November): 1433–37.

Schulberg, H. C., and E. Bromet. 1981. "Strategies for Evaluating the Outcome of Community Services for the Chronically Mentally Ill." *American Journal of Psychiatry* 138, no. 7 (July): 930–35.

Sorenson, J. E., and A. R. Kucic. 1981. "Assessing the Cost Outcomes and Cost Effectiveness of Community Support Programs (CSP): A Feasibility Study." Unpublished paper, University of Denver. Denver, Colorado.

Stroul, B.; L. Morrison; M. Kotler; and P. Rienzo. 1980. "Final Report of the Exploratory Evaluation of the National Institute of Mental Health Community Support Program." Silver Spring, Md.: Macro Systems, Inc.

Turner, J. C., and W. J. TenHoor. 1978. "The NIMH Community Support Program: Pilot Approach to a Needed Social Reform." *Schizophrenia Bulletin* 4, no. 3: 319–48.

Wholey, J. S. 1979. *Evaluation: Promise and Performance.* Washington, D.C.: The Urban Institute.

THE PROGRAM

3 PROGRAM DESCRIPTION AND LOGIC

The purpose of the present chapter is to describe the Community Support Program (CSP) in some detail and, in so doing, to explain its logic and intent. The program is best conceived in terms of its basic resources, activities, and objectives. Program resources consist of staff and money; both have expanded since the program's inception in 1977. As will be described later in the chapter, the CSP's activities are extremely varied. Among the activities prescribed by the program are advocacy, interagency collaboration, technical assistance, dissemination of information, and contract monitoring. A common set of objectives, involving the development of community support systems (CSSs), lends meaning and coherence to these varied activities and gives direction to the use of program resources. The CSP is at least as much a "program of influence," designed to stimulate changes in the system of care, as it is a program which provides direct client services. As shall be described later in this chapter, the program's sense of its unique mission has led it to focus its efforts very broadly and to invest resources and initiate distinct activities at the federal, state, and local levels.

This chapter is based, in part, on an NIMH document describing CSP principles and guidelines and, in part, on the Final Report of the Exploratory Evaluation of CSP, prepared by Beth Stroul, Lanny Morrison, Martin Kotler and Phyllis Rienzo of Macro Systems, Inc.

THE POPULATION OF CONCERN

The CSP focuses on adults eighteen years of age and over with severe mental or emotional disorders that impair their ability to function independently in community settings. The program is not intended for people who *appropriately* require long-term care in a hospital or nursing home. Nor is the program intended for people whose primary disability results from mental retardation, alcoholism, or drug abuse. Individuals falling within the purview of the CSP typically have undergone intensive psychiatric treatment more than once in a lifetime; some of these individuals have experienced structured psychiatric care during much of their adult lives (NIMH 1980).

In addition, such individuals are often unemployed and have markedly limited skills and a poor work history. Many of them require public financial assistance in order to live in the community, and may be unable to procure such assistance without outside help. Often the client lacks close friends and family, and may need help to establish or maintain a personal support system. Other characteristics of the population of concern include deficiencies in basic living skills, and inappropriate social behaviors that sometimes disturb other community residents. Based on the estimates developed for the National Plan for the Chronically Mentally Ill (NP/CMI), the population ranges from 800,000 to 1.5 million individuals in the United States. The range reflects measures of moderate as well as severe disability (Goldman, Gattozzi, and Taube 1981).

It is instructive to differentiate the activities of the CSP vis-a-vis this target population in terms of those which occur at the federal level (at NIMH), those which occur at the state level (State Mental Health Agencies), and those which occur at the level of the local community (CSSs). The following sections describe these three distinct levels of CSP activity.

THE FEDERAL LEVEL

The Community Support and Rehabilitation Branch, NIMH, constitutes the locus of CSP responsibility at the federal level. During the first three years of the program, under authority of

Sections 301 and 303(a)(2) of the Public Health Service Act, this branch invited applications for support of Strategy Development and Implementation projects, and Demonstration and Program Development projects.[1] During the initial three years, CSP contracted with a total of twenty states.[2] Through these contracts, the CSP sought to channel resources to states in order to further CSP goals and objectives.

Accordingly, a major set of activities at the federal level focuses on contractor selection and monitoring. Once a contract is awarded, it is the responsibility of the CSP Implementation Section to monitor project performance in accordance with a variety of project-reporting requirements.

NIMH also provides various forms of technical assistance to funded as well as non-funded projects: NIMH convenes periodic CSP Learning Community Conferences bringing together federal, state and local program planners, administrators, policymakers, direct service workers, and consumer representatives. Federal officials also prepare and disseminate technical materials to guide program development. In addition, federal program staff provide telephone assistance and conduct site visits to state and local projects.

At the federal level, additional resources are focused on advocacy and interagency collaboration. To advocate for the chronically mentally ill, NIMH disseminates information about the needs of the target population. A wide range of interest and constituency groups including consumers, former patients, and concerned parents are involved in this process. To promote interagency collaboration, the federal CSP office seeks the cooperation of key health, rehabilitation, housing, and other human service agencies who share responsibility for meeting the comprehensive needs of the target population. In summary, federal level activities focus primarily on contractor selection and monitoring, technical assistance, advocacy, and interagency collaboration on behalf of the chronically mentally ill.

THE STATE LEVEL

Four general types of coordination and system-building activities are required at the state level. These are (1) to maintain or improve state-level CSS program development capacity, (2) to assure broad-based participation in CSS decisionmaking, (3) to analyze available data on CSS needs and resources, and (4) to design and implement state CSS strategies. Each of these activities will be described in the present section.[3]

Effective CSS planning and implementation requires establishing a focal point within the state mental health agency for initiating and coordinating CSS-related activities. Each state project must establish a CSS staff which includes, at a minimum, a full-time project director responsible for managing activites undertaken in connection with the project. This person (or unit) is to be located in a position of "maximum organizational effectiveness" to coordinate CSS-related activities within the state mental health agency, and to collaborate with other state-level health and human service agencies (both public and private) whose programs may potentially benefit CSS clients.

Viable CSS strategies require the active support of a broad-based constituency. Accordingly, each state project should assess whether appropriate constituencies are being adequately informed and consulted about critical decisions related to CSS planning, policymaking, and budgeting. Where appropriate constituencies are not already involved, steps are to be taken to ensure broad-based participation by consumer, ex-patient, parent, professional, and paraprofessional groups to help formulate and advocate for statewide policies and programs for people with chronic mental illness.

Effective CSS strategies must also be based on a comprehensive understanding of current problems, and on careful assessments of the relative merits of alternative approaches. Therefore, it is necessary to periodically review and analyze currently available data on statewide CSS needs and resources as a basis for establishing specific objectives and priorities. More specifically, it is hoped that the review and analysis of available data will result in accurate estimates of the numbers, demographic and socioeconomic characteristics, current and projected location, and current and projected service needs of the CSS population. It is important that such analyses take into account information on the number and location of racial and ethnic minority group members of the CSS population so that the unique needs and special concerns of these clients can be met. It is also important to assess existing information on how the resources of the mental health and human services systems (both public and private) are currently being used to meet the needs of CSS clients. A major product should be a preliminary analysis of CSS problems and gaps, and priorities for CSS initiatives.

The fourth basic activity at the state level is to design and implement CSS strategies on a statewide basis. Generally, the strategies will consist of specific steps to be taken to fill gaps, improve coordination, upgrade quality and appropriateness, improve use of currently available resources, overcome or remove obstacles, maximize opportunities, and extend needed services to greater numbers of CSS clients. The specific strategies selected, the level of effort devoted to each, and the timing and sequencing of various activities will depend on circumstances specific to each state. At a minimum, however, it is expected that actions will be taken to modify and refine state mental health policy to promote CSS goals, and to collaborate with other state-level health and human service agencies including those responsible for health, medical assistance, income maintenance, social services, vocational rehabilitation, employment, housing, and transportation. It is also important to identify the technical assistance needs of a variety of organizations and agencies that serve, or should serve, CSS clients and, based on a general assessment of their needs, provide appropriate information and consultation to these groups. Finally, it is important to document statewide experiences in CSS development and, where possible, to identify the implications for future policy and practice.

THE LOCAL LEVEL

According to CSP guidelines, it is essential that ten CSS components be in place at the local level. These ten essential components are reproduced below from the NIMH Definition and Guiding Principles for Community Support Systems (1980).

1. *Locate CSS clients, reach out to inform them of available services,* and assure their access to needed services and community resources by arranging for transportation, if necessary, or by taking the services to clients.

2. *Help CSS clients meet basic human needs* for food, clothing, shelter, personal safety, general medical and dental care, and assist them to apply for income, medical, housing and/or other benefits which they may need and to which they are entitled.

3. *Provide adequate mental health care*, including diagnostic evaluation; prescription, periodic review and regulation of psychotropic drugs, as needed; and community-based psychiatric, psychological and/or counseling and treatment services.

4. *Provide 24-hour, quick response crisis assistance*, directed toward enabling both the client and involved family and friends to cope with emergencies, while maintaining the client's status as a functioning community member to the greatest extent possible. This should include round-the-clock telephone service, on call trained personnel, and options for either short-term or partial hospitalization or temporary supervised community housing arrangements.

5. *Provide comprehensive psychosocial services* which include a continuum of high to low expectation services and environments designed to improve or maintain clients' abilities to function in normal social roles. Some of these services should be available on an indefinite duration basis, and should include, but need not be limited to services which:

   a. *Help clients evaluate their strengths and weaknesses* and participate in setting their own goals and planning for appropriate services.

   b. *Train clients in daily and community living skills* such as medication use, diet, exercise, personal hygiene, shopping, cooking, budgeting, housekeeping, use of transportation, and other community resources. Whenever possible, these should be taught in the natural setting.

   c. *Help clients develop social skills, interests and leisure time activities* to provide a sense of participation and personal worth, including opportunities for age-appropriate, culturally appropriate daytime and evening activities.

   d. *Help clients find and make use of appropriate employment opportunities*, vocational rehabilitation services, or other supported or sheltered work environments. Provision must also be made for people who may not be able to use these opportunities and services, but who need a chance to be useful and a meaningful way to structure their time.

6. *Provide a range of rehabilitative and supportive housing options* for persons not in crisis who need a special living arrangement. The choices should be broad enough to allow each client an op-

portunity to live in an atmosphere offering the degree of support necessary while also providing incentives and encouragement for clients to assume increasing responsibility for their lives. Some supportive living arrangements must be available on an indefinite duration basis.

7. *Offer backup support, assistance, consultation and education* to families, friends, landlords, employers, community agencies and others who come in frequent contact with mentally disabled persons, to maximize benefits and minimize problems associated with the presence of these persons in the community.

8. *Recognize natural support systems,* such as neighborhood networks, churches, community organizations, commerce and industry, and encourage them to increase opportunities for mentally disabled persons to participate in community life.

9. *Establish grievance procedures and mechanisms to protect client rights,* both in and outside of mental health or residential facilities.

10. *Facilitate effective use by clients of formal and informal helping systems,* by designating a single person or team responsible for helping the client make informed choices about opportunities and services, assuring timely access to needed assistance, providing opportunities and encouragement for self-help activities, and coordinating all services to meet the client's goals.

In order to constitute a system, the ten components identified above must be integrated into a pattern of services that seeks to meet clients' needs and develop their potentials in a way that is flexible and holistic. To accomplish this goal, there must be systematic arrangements for program planning, development, monitoring, and evaluation. Responsibility for specific actions also needs to be identified and fixed at all levels (that is, the state, substate, catchment, and program levels). The NIMH Definition and Guiding Principles for CSSs further suggest that a "core service agency" be designated to act as a catalyst in developing and improving community support services. In addition, there must be a variety of other local programs available—programs which have adequate mandates, resources, and qualified staff to perform needed CSS functions.

At the client level, there should be an individual or team responsible for remaining in contact with the client on a continuing basis, whether the client is in the hospital or in the community and regardless of the number of agencies involved.[4] The number of clients assigned to this person or team should be small enough so that each client is known well and treated uniquely, and so that a supportive and caring relationship is possible. CSS guidelines also suggest that services to clients be guided by such basic principles as personal dignity, self-determination, least restrictive setting, and consumer and community involvement.[5]

THE EVALUABILITY ASSESSMENT

The next section describes the Evaluability Assessment (EA) process, which was initiated in October 1979, and completed in June 1980.[6] Also known as an "Exploratory Evaluation," the overall goal is to develop an "evaluable" program, that is, a program in which objectives are clearly specified and agreed upon at all levels of management and policymaking, underlying causal assumptions are explicitly stated, specific indicators of program accomplishment are identified and agreed upon, and intended uses of evaluative information are defined in advance of data collection. It is hoped that the EA will help to clarify each of these issues and in so doing put program evaluation on a track that is sound, relevant, and potentially useful.

The EA process is unique in that it requires evaluators to work closely with program managers. Throughout the process, evaluators work with management to clarify and describe the program's design and operation. In order to ensure programmatic input and feedback at each stage in the process, EAs are conducted by a work group consisting of program representatives and evaluators.[7] Also, substantive input and direction are obtained by convening a policy group consisting of key program managers and policymakers.[8]

The EA of the CSP involved the accomplishment of four broad tasks: (1) documenting the intended program, (2) documenting the actual program, (3) analyzing and synthesizing findings and formulating preliminary evaluation-management options, and (4) reanalyzing and reformulating feasible evaluation-management options based upon feedback from the policy group. The present chapter focuses on the first two of these tasks. Discussion of tasks (3) and (4) will be taken up in Chapter 4.

The EA methodology calls for the use of models to define and depict central aspects of the program. One type of model, the logic model, seeks to represent, in a graphic format, the logical structure of the intended program in terms of its inputs, activities, and expected results with a clear presentation of the logic of the causal assumptions linking these different program elements. The logic model is generally presented as a series of events occurring in a logical sequence that lead (theoretically) to the achievement of the program objectives. Logic models provide a basis for assessing whether program objectives and related activities are well defined, and for assessing the plausibility and feasibility of the program logic. The next section describes the specific steps we took to analyze the logic of the CSP.

DOCUMENTING THE INTENDED PROGRAM

In order to determine management's objectives for the program, as well as the objectives of other individuals in policymaking positions, two specific steps were taken. First, available documentation pertinent to the intent of the program was reviewed, and summary reports were prepared. Second, key program managers and policymakers were interviewed. These were individuals who were currently or historically involved with CSP, and included three CSP managers, five individuals at other management and policymaking levels in NIMH, congressional committee staff, and representatives of six key interest groups and professional associations. Information was obtained regarding their perspectives on CSP's major activities and resources, purposes and objectives, expectations, program performance information, and problems which the program faced.

To further reduce this volume of information, logic models were developed. As previously described, these models seek to represent graphically the logical structure of the intended program in terms of its resource inputs, activities, and expected outcomes. The elements are linked by arrows reflecting the progression from inputs to activities to intermediate and long-range objectives.

Three logic models of CSP were constructed at varying levels of complexity. We shall focus on the Level II model, shown in

Figure 3–1. Reading from left to right, one can see the progression from input to activities to expected results. Activities are separated into those occurring at the federal level and those occurring at the state and/or local levels. Expected results are grouped into intermediate system change objectives, and longer range objectives for services and clients.

The CSP input elements include the legislative authority for the program, amount and source of funds, the program's place in the organizational (bureaucratic) hierarchy, and other bases for the program including the General Accounting Office's report, the President's Commission on Mental Health, and the CSS concept development and planning processes initiated by NIMH in 1974.

CSP activities at the federal level are depicted in relation to four distinct categories: (1) contracts with states, (2) technical assistance, (3) interagency collaboration, and (4) advocacy. State and local efforts emanating from these federal activities are summarized in the next boxes. They include the creation of a locus of responsibility for CSS activities at the state level, the formulation of a statewide planning effort, and the development of model CSSs.

Following the logical sequence of the model, it can be stated that *if* the prescribed activities occur at the federal, state, and local levels, *then* the program's objectives should be met. Based on analysis of written documentation and interview data, six basic objectives of the CSP were derived. They are:

1. *Quality of Life/Client Objectives*—Reflect the notion that all CSP activity is ultimately for the purpose of improving the quality of the lives of chronically mentally ill people.
2. *Service Delivery Objectives*—Include objectives relative to the development of comprehensive CSSs, with their ten essential service components as well as those relating to the general improvement of opportunities, resources, services, and service delivery for the chronically mentally ill.
3. *State Responsibility/Leadership Objectives*—Reflect the effort by NIMH to assist State Mental Health Agencies to assume the responsibility for (and leadership in) meeting the needs of the chronically mentally ill.
4. *Stimulation/Influence Objectives*—Reflect the perception of CSP as a "program of influence." These objectives reflect the

CSP's intention to encourage other health and human service agencies at all levels of government to give higher priority to the needs of the chronically mentally ill.

5. *Technology/Learning Objectives*—Capture the pilot concept of CSP by emphasizing the importance of advancing the state of the art on how to most effectively plan, organize, finance, monitor, evaluate, and deliver community support services, and how most effectively to organize the various services into functioning CSSs.

6. *Resources Objectives*—Include the concept that the use of mainstream state and federal resources should be maximized in the development and long-term support of CSSs and that better use should be made of existing available resources to which the target population may be entitled.

In the logic model, these objectives (or intended results) are sequenced from the intermediate to the longer range. The sequencing of elements in the logic model also reflects a progression from the systems level to the client level. Although achievement of both types of objectives may occur simultaneously, the systems results can be viewed as precursors to (or facilitative conditions for) results at the client level. The linkages between elements in the logic model reflect a series of causal assumptions. These assumptions form the basis of the program's logic and reflect the belief that, *IF* specific activities occur at the federal, state, and local levels, *THEN* CSP's objectives will be achieved. Analysis of these IF-THEN hypotheses helps to clarify the assumptions which underlie the program strategy. Key IF-THEN propositions include the following:

1. If NIMH contracts with states for CSS strategy development, then states will assume leadership roles in planning for the statewide development of CSSs.

2. If NIMH contracts with states for CSS demonstration and program development, then states will refine and develop local CSSs.

3. If NIMH provides technical assistance, then CSS-related activities will be facilitated.

4. If NIMH, in conjunction with a range of special interest and constituency groups, advocates for the needs of the target

Figure 3–1.   Community Support Program Logic—Level II.

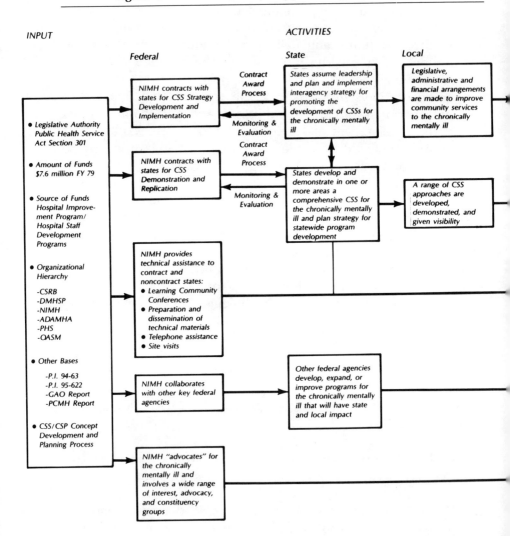

Source: Stroul, Morrison, Kotler, and Rienzo. (1980: II-10).

OBJECTIVES/RESULTS

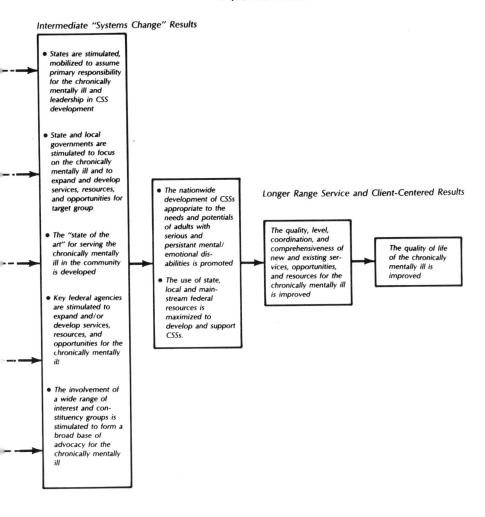

Intermediate "Systems Change" Results

- States are stimulated, mobilized to assume primary responsibility for the chronically mentally ill and leadership in CSS development

- State and local governments are stimulated to focus on the chronically mentally ill and to expand and develop services, resources, and opportunities for target group

- The "state of the art" for serving the chronically mentally ill in the community is developed

- Key federal agencies are stimulated to expand and/or develop services, resources, and opportunities for the chronically mentally ill

- The involvement of a wide range of interest and constituency groups is stimulated to form a broad base of advocacy for the chronically mentally ill

- The nationwide development of CSSs appropriate to the needs and potentials of adults with serious and persistant mental/emotional disabilities is promoted

- The use of state, local and mainstream federal resources is maximized to develop and support CSSs.

Longer Range Service and Client-Centered Results

The quality, level, coordination, and comprehensiveness of new and existing services, opportunities, and resources for the chronically mentally ill is improved

The quality of life of the chronically mentally ill is improved population, then other federal agencies will collaborate in developing and expanding opportunities for the chronically mentally ill in the community.

The next hypothesis considers the joint effect of the prior events in affecting intermediate system changes:

5. If NIMH contracts with states, provides technical assistance, and joins in an advocacy effort on behalf of the target population, and if the prescribed federal, state, and local activities ensue, then:
   - State governments will assume increasing responsibility for the chronically mentally ill and leadership in CSS development.
   - There will be advances in the state-of-the-art for serving the chronically mentally ill.
   - Non-mental health agencies at the federal, state, and local levels will take an increasing role in delivering services and providing resources and opportunities for the target population.

The next objectives, which depend on the realization of all prior conditions, constitute the long-term goals of the CSP:

6. If all of the above occur, then the nationwide development of CSSs for the chronically mentally ill will have been promoted.
7. If CSSs are developed, then the quality, level, coordination, and comprehensiveness of services for the chronically mentally ill will be improved.
8. If the quality, level, coordination, and comprehensiveness of services, opportunities, and resources are improved, then the quality of life of the chronically mentally ill will improve.

In summary, this section has described the objectives and logic of the CSP from the perspective of the program managers and policymakers. The analysis is cast in terms of causal linkages between resource inputs, federal-state-local activities, and expected outcomes. It is noteworthy that little disagreement existed among the individuals interviewed by the work group about the program's basic activities or objectives. While there was some tendancy to assign different priorities to different components of the program, there was notable consonance in the descriptive material generated by the interviews, which formed the basis for the logic model.

DOCUMENTING THE ACTUAL PROGRAM

In the prior section we analyzed the federal *intent* of the CSP from the perspective of program managers and policymakers. In the present section, we examine the program from the perspective of the staff in the field—that is, through the eyes of individuals who are actually working in the state and local projects. We are interested in whether, and to what extent, the perception of the program in the field parallels the federal intent, as depicted in the logic model.

As a first step, documentation of all CSP projects was reviewed to develop a broader understanding of the range of activities and approaches in the field, and to develop a reasoned basis for the selection of sites to visit. For this purpose, the first-year technical proposals and year-end final reports for all CSP projects were reviewed. Based on this review, the work group identified and abstracted information pertinent to fifteen classification criteria to describe project characteristics. Six of these criteria were subsequently used to select a sample for field visiting. These were: (1) contract type and year, (2) NIMH funding rank in the first year, (3) region of country, (4) urban-rural character of demonstration area, (5) population size of demonstration area, and (6) type of core service agency. Sites for further study were then selected with the objective of capturing the diversity among CSP projects so that the field visits would be representative.

Field visits to seven states were conducted over a span of three weeks, using two-person teams.[9] Approximately eighty-five individuals were interviewed in total. The sites visited included four regional ADAMHA offices (Regions II, IV, VIII, I, and X), six state offices (Massachusetts, Montana, Oregon, Colorado, Georgia, and Florida), and five local projects (Massachusetts, Montana, Colorado, Florida, and New York). At the regional offices, the work group interviewed the regional CSP consultant-coordinator and the ADAMHA division director. At the state offices, the work group interviewed the state-level CSP project director, key project personnel, and others knowledgeable about project issues, operations, and expected results. At the local demonstration sites, we interviewed the local program director, administrator, and other staff members responsible for key program activities.

In the interviews we sought to elicit statements of project objectives, descriptions of major project activities, and potential as well as currently available measures of project performance and accomplishments. Additional questions focused on operating assumptions, problems-barriers, and system interrelationships describing relations among state-level CSP projects, regional office, NIMH, and other key actors-agencies in the environment in which the project operates.

Field visit reports were prepared in the form of interview summaries. A content analysis of the data revealed a high level of agreement between federal intent (as described in the logic model) and the actual activities in the field. Although the site visits did reveal some differences in emphasis and approach, the work group on the whole was impressed with the shared understandings that exist at all levels concerning program inputs, activities, and objectives. In brief, it appears that CSP is a national program around which broad consensus exists among the participants and policymakers and there is little divergence among project staff at federal, regional, state, and local levels in their definitions of, or expectations for, the program. However self-selection bias could account for the high level of agreement. State projects were selected for funding by NIMH program staff, in part, for congruence with federal intentions.

CONCLUSION

Based on the EA, we conclude that the program makes logical sense "on paper," and it appears that a good match exists between federal intent and the CSP activities that are actually underway at the state and local levels. But are there logical flaws, implausibilities, and infeasibilities? Will the model demonstrations be generalizable? Do the basic principles work in the current settings-contexts? What evidence is there from other programs predicated on similar logic? The next chapter focuses on these questions in considerable detail.

NOTES

1. Beginning in September 1980, CSP began shifting from a program of contracts to a program of grants. This change in funding mechanism was necessary in order for NIMH to comply with the Federal Grant and Cooperative Agreement Act of 1977.

2. The eight states participating in the program through Strategy Development and Implementation contracts were: Alabama, Arizona, Georgia, Maine, Maryland, New Jersey, Ohio, and Oregon. The twelve states participating in the program through Demonstration and Program Development contracts were: California, Colorado, District of Columbia, Florida, Massachusetts, Michigan, Minnesota, Missouri, Montana, New York, South Dakota, and Texas. In fiscal year 1979, the budget for contracts with states was $7.6 million.

3. This section draws upon the September 1980 NIMH Grant Announcement, entitled "Community Support Systems Strategy Development and Implementation Grants." Catalogue of Federal Domestic Assistance 13.242 Mental Health Research Grants. It should be recognized that the 1980 grant announcement also revised the program guidelines. It rearranged the ten components, combined state and local programs into a single "Strategy Development and Implementation Grant," provided a slightly revised definition of the target population, and identified revised activities to be undertaken.

4. This function is variously referred to as "case management" or "resource management."

5. A complete list of the guiding principles, along with a brief explanation of each, is included in the NIMH Definition and Guiding Principles for Community Support Systems (September, 1980).

6. Additional detail about the EA is available in the Final Report which was prepared by Macro Systems, Inc.: Beth Stroul, Lanny Morrison, Martin Kotler, and Phyllis Rienzo. Final Report of the Exploratory Evaluation of the National Institute of Mental Health Community Support Program, Macro Systems, Inc., June 30, 1980.

7. The EA of the CSP included the following persons on the work group: David Pharis (ASPE), John Sessler (OASH), Howard Goldman, Richard Tessler, Jacqueline Rosenberg, Robert Lilly

60 THE PROGRAM

(NIMH), Martin Kotler, Lanny Morrison, Beth Stroul, and Phyllis Rienzo (Macro Systems, Inc.).
8. The members of the policy group were Steven Sharfstein, Judith Turner, Irene Shifren, William TenHoor, Cecil Wurster, Beatrice Rosen, Richard Woy (NIMH), and Dennis Andrulis (ASPE).
9. Where possible, these two-person teams consisted of one person from the federal government and one person from Macro Systems, Inc.

REFERENCES

Goldman, H. H.; A. A. Gattozzi; and C. A. Taube. 1981. "Defining and Counting the Chronically Mentally Ill." *Hospital and Community Psychiatry* 32, no. 1 (January): 21–27.
National Institute of Mental Health. "NIMH Definition and Guiding Principles for Community Support Systems (CSSs)." September 1980. Rockville, Md.: Community Support and Rehabilitation Branch, Division of Mental Health Service Programs, NIMH.
Stroul, B.; L. Morrison, M. Kotler; and P. Rienzo. 1980. "Final Report of the Exploratory Evaluation of the National Institute of Mental Health Community Support Program." Silver Spring, Md.: Macro Systems, Inc.

4 PLAUSIBILITY

"Yes, But Will It Work?"

In the previous chapter, we detailed the objectives and logic of the Community Support Program (CSP); we modeled intended CSP activities; and we described what CSP field activities were like in reality. Our work group was impressed by the clarity with which the program intentions were articulated and by the apparent consistency between the structure and design of the intended and the actual program. Our next step was to determine if the program was plausible: Is it likely that the program activities will achieve progress toward objectives? Plausibility may be challenged by factors such as lack of resources, unrealistic schedules, lack of evidence that intended program activities are occurring, and lack of a theory or evidence that intended program activities have produced intended results in similar prior situations. This analysis was based on the information we detailed through interviews with program managers and policymakers, review of CSP documents, and field visits to program sites.

The plausibility analysis of CSP must be viewed in the context of the complexity of the problem CSP seeks to address, the com-

This chapter is adapted from a document entitled, "Final Report of the Exploratory Evaluation of the National Institute of Mental Health Community Support Program." June 30, 1980. Prepared by Beth Stroul, Lanny Morrison, Martin Kotler, and Phyllis Rienzo of Macro Systems, Inc.

plexity of the environment in which CSP operates, and the complexity of CSP itself. First, the complexity of serving the chronically mentally ill in the community is apparent in definitional problems related to both the target population and to services, and the lack of a clear-cut "technology" for effectively serving the chronically mentally ill. Uncertainty is inherent in addressing this problem—there are no clear-cut "cookbook" guidelines for what needs to be done and how it should be done.

Second, there are a number of other entities, factors, processes, and systems in addition to CSP that influence the program as it pursues its objectives. The overlap with and dependence upon the social service and health care delivery systems affect CSP's operations and results. Moreover, CSP is influenced by other mental health programs such as Community Mental Health Centers (CMHCs) and hospitals, by state legislatures and bureaucracies, and by general societal conditions such as the state of the economy and attitudes toward mental illness. Determining the extent to which CSP alone can be held accountable for its long-range objectives is difficult. Similarly, determining the extent to which changes in systems, services, and clients can be attributed reliably to CSP interventions is challenging.

Third, CSP has tackled a complex problem and has chosen to address it on a broad array of fronts, employing multilevel interventions and a wide range of strategies. A program with such diverse objectives is often seen as diffuse or not reducible to easily quantifiable variables. In such a program, a conflict may arise between demonstrating progress toward intermediate or "process" objectives and achieving longer range outcomes. Managers, in particular, argue that achieving the intermediate systems change objective is as crucial as demonstrating the longer range improvements in services and clients. Many of the issues and questions raised by our analysis are inherent in CSP's broad and unique approach. Our task was to find the balance between idealistic objectives and achievable goals and to test the plausibility of CSP.

CSP PLAUSIBILITY ANALYSIS

The analysis is organized to present eight separate issues, with brief explanatory discussion of each and delineation of possible implications for program plausibility. Following discussion of each issue and its implications, some options for CSP management and policymakers to address the issues are delineated. Ultimately, the plausibility analysis should help to refine understanding of program objectives and to help plan future evaluations of the program.

CSP Resources are Inadequate to Achieve the Broad Range of Objectives

CSP, based upon the agreed-upon description of the intended program, encompasses a variety of multilevel interventions which address a broad array of objectives. Systems change outcomes are sought and these are assumed to lead sequentially to the development of Community Support Systems (CSSs), service improvement, and ultimately to improvement in the quality of life of the chronically mentally ill. According to early program rhetoric, CSP was originally conceptualized as a pilot program primarily for the purpose of focusing attention on the chronic population, stimulating systems to be more responsive to the population's needs and demonstrating effective approaches. The intended program, however, specifies *nationwide* development of CSSs, service improvement, and improvement of the quality of life of the target population as its long-range objectives.

At the time of the analysis, CSP contracted with nineteen states, with a total of $7.6 million supporting CSP field activities. This level of resources and activity is not adequate to achieve the longer range objectives on a nationwide basis, for example, improvement of the quality of life of the chronically mentally ill nationwide. The likelihood of achieving long-range CSP objectives diminishes given the present level of resources.

CSP managers and policymakers sought to improve the likelihood of achieving the long-range objectives by demonstrating the viability of the CSS approach and focusing attention and priority on the target group, thus generating demand for more programs and services of a similar nature. In addition, a CSP hypothesis was that through strategic placement of relatively modest federal resources, state, local, and mainstream federal resources could be accessed to develop and support CSSs. This hypothesis has yet to be proven, and the shift to a block grant approach to federal funding of mental health programs provides the ultimate test of the influence of CSP and the viability of its CSS approach.

CSP might have chosen to promote the development of CSSs on a nationwide basis without the application of *any* additional categorical resources to states and localities. To some extent, CSP has attempted to influence nonfunded entities, for example, by inviting nonfunded states to Learning Community Conferences and through the diffusion of CSS concepts and ideas. Theoretically, it might be possible to exert influence on the nature of the service systems by acting solely as an information broker and an advocate. The plausibility, however, of achieving demonstratable changes toward CSP objectives within a reasonable time frame without providing resources to support efforts in the desired directions is questionable.

CSP managers and policymakers recognized that additional resources would be needed for full nationwide achievement of the long-range goals, and their standards and expectations for achievement have been lowered with respect to progress toward the long-range goals depicted in the model. For our analysis, it is important to maintain the intended program description as delineated in Chapter 3 since it does reflect CSP's ultimate goals, and would likely be the basic design of an expanded effort on behalf of the target group. The work group concluded:

1. The current level of resources is not adequate for full achievement of CSP's objectives on a nationwide basis.
2. If, for accountability purposes, CSP focuses on the intermediate objectives plus achieving service and client changes at demonstration and replication sites, the likelihood of success is improved. With this emphasis, resources are more likely to be deemed adequate and this particular plausibility issue may be diminished.

They outlined the following:

1. Seek additional resources to expand CSP to a nationwide effort.
2. Although management is reluctant to do so, the program description could be modified to reflect more modest goals.
3. Hold CSP accountable for achieving its objectives only in funded States and its long-range objectives only at demonstration and program development sites. At this time, evaluation would be fo-

cused only on funded entities. This evaluation of the "pilot" CSP effort would involve testing the viability and success of the approach, and could serve as justification for an expanded effort. Assuming the program gets additional resources, evaluation activities can then be expanded.

It is Questionable whether CSP Objectives can be Achieved without Significant Categorical Federal Support

The implementation of the types of service systems envisioned by CSP depends largely on the use of mainstream federal, state, local and other resources. The CSP hypothesis is that resources can probably be redirected, that adequate mainstream resources are probably available to develop and support comprehensive service systems for the target group, and that major infusions of new categorical federal mental health funds may not be necessary. The hypothesis includes the notion that these resources could be accessed-redirected through strategic placement of "front-end" federal resources to initiate activities which can then generate ongoing support.

There are caps, however, on many of the mainstream resources that CSP seeks to tap. It is therefore questionable whether mainstream resources are present in sufficient quantity or diversity to provide the ten CSS components. Further, much depends upon state and local willingness to commit resources to the care of the chronically mentally ill, which is questionable in some states and localities, particularly in an atmosphere of fiscal conservatism. In addition, CSP moneys have supported state-level CSP initiatives and *services* at demonstration sites. There is much concern in the field about whether states and communities will fund those state-level activities and services when federal support terminates.

The work group listed two major implications of this issue:

1. It may not be possible to sustain State-level CSP efforts and momentum or to continue critical local CSS services at demonstration sites at the current level when Federal support terminates.
2. The hypothesis that CSSs can be developed and supported primarily with State, local, and mainstream Federal resources is

questionable. The early experience of CSP regarding the use of front-end money to access stable long-term support has not yet been evaluated. Unless evidence is obtained to support the plausibility of this approach, CSP objectives may not be achievable without significant Federal categorical support.

The basic hypothesis can be tested by (1) studying the applicability and availability of mainstream programs to the chronically mentally ill, (2) assessing the extent to which state and local CSP projects have accessed state, local and mainstream federal resources, and (3) evaluating the ability and plans of state and local projects to continue activities and services when federal support terminates. Information of this nature is critically important for future management decisionmaking regarding the viability of the current CSP approach.

The Efficacy of the Service Coordination-Collaboration Approach is Questionable

The CSS concept and its components are based on the recognition that the chronically mentally ill have a range of needs that cannot all be met by the mental health system in isolation (e.g., vocational rehabilitation, housing with varying degrees of supervision, social services, health care). The fragmentation of the health, mental health, and social service delivery systems is also recognized as a problem. CSP was designed to fix responsibility for the target population at federal, state and local levels and to create a network or system through which comprehensive services can be provided to mentally disabled adults. The basic mechanism to overcome fragmentation and to access services, resources, and opportunities for the target group is interagency collaboration at each level. CSP has sought interagency agreements and other working arrangements at federal, state, and local levels to obtain those services and resources needed by the target group and to coordinate service delivery more effectively.

There is little evidence to support the efficacy of a service coordination-collaboration approach to address the fragmentation of the service delivery system. A number of previous programs have been conceived and implemented using a services-integration model (Gray Areas, Model Cities, SITO, Hartford Experiment, OEO, etc.). There is little evidence that these prototypes have succeeded in achieving their stated purposes. In addition, a number of problems surrounding interagency collaboration in CSP have been observed through field visits and interviews with managers and policymakers: (1) Historically, there has been resistance and lack of commitment of some mainstream agencies to serve the chronically mentally ill. Interagency collaboration efforts at each level have been largely voluntary and persuasive processes. It has been especially difficult to persuade, cajole, and convince agency policymakers to take action on behalf of the chronically mentally ill if they have no clear mandate or authority to do so. (2) There is a tendency at each level (federal, state, substate regional, and local) to think that collaborative activities are more appropriate and efficacious at another level and should be someone else's major responsibility. (3) There is a widespread belief that many of the meetings, agreements, and exchanges do not result in identifiable benefits for service delivery and for clients. As a result, overwhelming problems and obstacles have been encountered when trying to negotiate interagency activities on behalf of the target group.

The work group concluded:

Interagency collaboration may not be a plausible approach for addressing the fragmentation of the health, mental health, and social service delivery systems. CSP was somewhat different from previous initiatives in that a point of responsibility for interagency activities was established at each level. Although the array of problems and obstacles involved in the approach may impede the achievement of CSP objectives, there may not be any viable alternate approaches to obtain the requisite services and resources for the chronically mentally ill. Options include:

1. Identify realistic leverage points (e.g., legislation or financial incentives) to ensure the effectiveness of interagency activities; identify mechanisms to induce or to provide conditions conducive to obtaining the cooperation of key agencies. States could assist in the identification of potential leverage points and strategies for overcoming the problems involved in voluntary interagency collaboration.
2. Clarify the interagency collaboration process including the responsibilities for such efforts at Federal, State and local efforts; suggest priority areas for interagency efforts.
3. Identify alternative approaches to access requisite resources and services for the target population.

The Causal Link between Multiple Systems Changes and Service Improvement and Client-Related Outcomes Needs to be Tested

The CSP logic model depicts the assumption that achieving the intermediate, systems change objectives will lead to the accomplishment of longer term objectives (CSS development, service improvements, and quality of life improvement). This is, in fact, the major hypothesis of the CSP effort. The program intent is to demonstrate that there is such a causal link and to refine the strategy to determine and demonstrate *which* systems changes are highly correlated with actual changes in services, and ultimately, in clients. It is unclear, however, whether there is evidence to support this hypothesis. In fact, there may be evidence to the contrary when other systems change efforts are examined. The work group concluded:

1. The hypothesis that systems changes will result in actual beneficial changes in services and ultimately in desired client outcomes needs testing.
2. The lack of knowledge of which systems changes are correlated with actual changes in services and clients may result in misplaced CSP efforts at all levels.

And two recommendations were made:

1. Begin the methodological and exploratory work necessary to test this hypothesis, including (1) operationalizing the systems change objectives, (2) development of reliable and valid outcome measures, and (3) pilot testing methodological tools.
2. Begin to identify those systems changes which seem correlated with service improvement and focus CSP efforts in these directions.

The Role of CSP Relative to the Existing Mental Health System is not Clear

The role and objectives of CSP vis-á-vis the rest of the existing mental health system (state hospitals and community-based services) is not clearly articulated in the description of the intended program. Some policymakers and others at state and regional levels view community support services as added interventions missing from the existing mental health system and suggest that additional resources would enable mental health programs and facilities to serve the chronically mentally ill more comprehensively and appropriately. The importance of a visible initiative to focus attention on the target group, to stimulate changes in the system, and to develop and demonstrate effective approaches to serving the chronically mentally ill has been underscored by many of those interviewed for exploratory evaluation purposes. At the same time, a major objective of CSP is conceptualized by many interviewees as making the existing mental health system (e.g., CMHCs and psychiatric hospitals) more responsive to the target group in more appropriate ways. Many states explicitly mentioned this as a major objective of their CSP projects. This objective, however, is not explicit or operationally defined in CSP's program description.

Just as the role, relationship and objectives of CSP regarding the existing mental health system have been unclear, CSP's role in relation to the Mental Health Systems Act (MHSA) and the National Plan for the Chronically Mentally Ill (NP/CMI) were never clearly specified. Senate and House versions of the MHSA differed in designation of primary responsibility for the target population, in the nature of proposed initiatives for the target population, and in the locus of administration of community mental health (including community support) programs. The final MHSA reflected a compromise. The NP/CMI, broader in scope than CSP, provided an overall framework for comprehensive services to the target group. How the CSP approach, concepts, and components fit into the implementation of the new federal block grant program remains to be seen. Attending to the current mental health system, however, is critical to the success of the CSP.

Although CSP seeks to have an impact beyond the mental health system, the current mental health system's structure and facilities play a key role in CSP efforts. The state mental health authorities are the focal point of responsibility for the target population; changes in state hospitals are imperative for successful deinstitutionalization and community support efforts; local mental health agencies (CMHCs, freestanding mental health clinics, local hospitals) are operational in many areas and are seen as responsible for serving the target group. Although CSP did not seek to create a new and separate system, CSP's role, relationships, and objectives regarding the existing system have not been specified.

The work group found that:

1. The lack of clearly defined relationships and goals regarding the existing mental health system may impede the achievement of CSP's objectives.
2. Turf-guarding, competition, and resistance may result from the lack of clarity, rather than coordinated efforts at all levels.
3. Some existing mental health programs may see CSP as an excuse to avoid redefining their programs and priorities and provide comprehensive services to the chronic population.
4. It remains unclear whether the CSP program intends to continue as a separate Federal initiative, or whether it will eventually be subsumed under a different aegis. [Block grants will clearly force this decision in the latter direction.]

It follows, then, that CSP might seek to:

1. Improve the lines of communication and the coordination of activity between CSP and other mental health entitites (CMHCs, State hospitals, etc.) at Federal, Regional ADAMHA, and State levels.
2. Clarify the roles of CMHCs and State hospitals as part of (or in relation to) CSSs.
3. Clarify CSP's role and objectives vis-á-vis the existing mental health system.

Analysis and Dissemination of the Existing Body of Knowledge and Experience has not been Occurring, Primarily Due to a Lack of Resources for this Function

Since CSP was originally conceptualized as a pilot program, development and dissemination of the state of the art were considered of major importance. Analysis of the experiences of states and communities in developing and organizing CSSs and in providing community support services is a key element in the intended program. This is reflected in a specific objective of the federal program which reflects the intention to "develop the state of the art for serving the chronically mentally ill in the community," that is, to develop and disseminate CSS implementation, operation, and evaluation strategies; to develop and disseminate methods, models and materials; to collectively analyze the experience and identify successful and less successful approaches; and to clarify CSS implications for policy, practice, and resources at all levels. However, due to lack of resources and the necessity for managing the CSP contracts, this activity has not been implemented at the federal level to the extent necessary for achieving the objective. Due to the pilot nature of the program, the importance of this element of the program description is magnified.

Without sufficient attention and resources devoted to the program analysis function, the work group reported:

1. CSP may institutionalize an approach or approaches 'before the returns are in.'
2. A body of knowledge and experience relative to CSSs would not be developed and disseminated, and the objective related to this would not be achieved.
3. The implications of the CSS approach for policy, practice, and resources at the Federal level would not be clarified, and there would be no clear basis for future program activity and directions.

It was suggested that CSP "design and implement a program analysis and dissemination function at the Federal level."

The Lack of a Well-Defined and Implemented Technical Assistance Function will Probably Impede the Achievement of CSP's Objectives.

We previously noted that activities related to the state-of-the-art development and dissemination were not implemented to the extent necessary to achieve program objectives. The technical assistance function was not well defined and was also not implemented to the extent necessary to achieve objectives. The need for more systematic and extensive technical assistance has been expressed frequently by state and localities.

The work group stated:

Without a well-articulated technical assistance function, with sufficient resources, the achievement of CSP's objectives probably will be impeded.

They recommended that the program develop this function along with its monitoring and evaluation functions. Furthermore, the advent of block grant funding and the shift of control over federal mental health resources to single state agencies will make technical assistance even more critical. In fact, technical assistance may remain as the sole federal role for CSP in the 1980s. Even evaluation may shift predominantly to the states with CSP and NIMH serving only as a clearinghouse for disseminating the results of state innovations and as a provider of assistance in the assessment of program performance. Success in fulfilling the CSP goal to promote the development of CSSs throughout the nation may depend on skilled technical assistance.

Due to a "Blurring" of the Two Types of CSP Contracts, There is a Discrepancy between the Intended Program Description and the Program Reality

Early CSP program rhetoric differentiates between the two types of CSP contracts—state strategy development and state-local CSS demonstration and replication. The two types of contracts represented two ways to approach CSS development: (1) by implementing a number of activities at the state level designed to promote CSS development and (2) by developing and demonstrating a comprehensive CSS to use as a basis for replication in other areas. The description of the intended program reflects the two distinct contract types. The two-headed arrow connecting the contract types (p. 54) represents the fact that the state-level activities occur under the demonstration contracts and that demonstration activities occur under the strategy-development contracts.

Observation of field operations revealed that, over time, the distinction between the contract types has blurred. This seems to be due to federal emphasis on state-level system change activity in both contract types, and the perceived need by most states to develop, demonstrate, and give visibility to CSSs or CSS components. The real differences between contract types were probably greater at the program's inception, and differences in emphasis may remain. However, the intended program description differentiates between contract types to an extent that is probably greater than the reality. In this sense, the description is no longer an accurate representation of field operations.

The work group suggested that future distinctions between the two contract types may not be necessary. Management may choose to offer grant support (as opposed to contract support) in only one major category thus eliminating the distinctions between the two current contract types. The grant program might include certain required activities or elements (e.g., state-level system intervention); other activity elements, such as demonstration projects, might be optional.

The work group concluded that a new CSP grant mechanism should be structured to facilitate achievement of CSP's intent. CSP has operated from its onset through contracts. The contract mechanism has allowed CSP to prescribe, with a great deal of specificity, the activities states are to perform and the information to be reported. Although shortages of staff have led to discontinuity of project officers and resultant discomfort among states, the procurement and contract monitoring processes have played a key role in shaping the implementation of the program toward CSP objectives. The shift to a grant mechanism necessitates careful design and articulation of guidelines, regulations, and grant award and monitoring processes in order to maintain CSP's ability to shape program implementation toward achieving its objectives and to learn from the grantee's experience. Without guideline and regulatory language that specifically addresses the activities grantees are to perform, the objectives and activities intended by CSP may not be realizable. Further, without specific guideline and regulatory language, it may not be possible to collect necessary data from grantees other than through special studies. Reasonable grant award and monitoring processes can also be designed to enhance CSP's ability to influence field operations.

Since the pilot experience of CSP as yet has not been fully analyzed and its hypotheses are largely untested, it would be premature to use the change in funding mechanism to change the basic nature, intent, or structure of the program. Although some clarification or modification may be desired by CSP management, it may be counterproductive to undertake any major changes in CSP intent, design, or premises until careful analysis and evaluation have been completed.

IMPLICATIONS

In an exploratory evaluation, a plausibility analysis has the potential to influence the program in three important ways: (1) Program managers might refine and restate program objectives to increase their plausibility, that is, the likelihood that program goals can be accomplished. (2) Program evaluators could focus their activities on helping to operationalize vague or complex objectives and on assessing the plausibility of assumptions linking program inputs and activities to program goals. (3) Policymakers might rethink the program "from the intent up," modifying objectives, assumptions, and program activities.

Major programmatic and policy alterations did not result immediately from the plausibility analysis and did not influence the main body of the evaluation of CSP. However, since the time of this investigation in 1979/80, there have been some significant policy changes. In Chapter 10, we will explore the policy implications of program plausibility and of the preliminary evaluation findings in the context of recent changes in federal mental health policy. Minor adjustments were made in the statement of program objectives, especially modifications based on the findings of this analysis.

The most important yield of the plausibility analysis was in the area of program evaluation. The analysis made several issues clear:

1. Intermediate systems change objectives ought to be a major focus of CSP evaluation, complementing the assessment of the impact of CSP on chronically mentally ill individuals.
2. The hypothesized link between intermediate systems change and client outcome must be investigated.

3. The use of mainstream resources by CSP programs and their clients must be carefully assessed.
4. The relationships between a CSS, the mental health system, the health, and social welfare systems must be defined and studied.

These evaluation imperatives, and the plausibility analysis which revealed them, also suggested several methodological problems. The work group identified three important measurement limitations impeding the evaluation of CSP: the lack of an agreed-upon and easily measured definition of the target population, difficulty in operationally defining the ten essential components of a CSS, and the absence of consensus on measures of program performance. These methodological limitations and the specific problems of evaluationg CSP on multiple levels became the object of considerable study. The efforts of CSP's evaluators were directed to meet these challenges. The next chapters discuss their research.

5 IMPLEMENTING STATE PROGRAMS

The present chapter considers the pilot experience of the Community Support Program (CSP) from the perspective of program staff in state mental health agencies. It is based on research visits in early 1981 by Macro Systems, Inc., to sites in Arizona, District of Columbia, Maine, Michigan, Minnesota, Missouri, New Jersey, South Dakota, and Texas, and is supplemented by review of program documents of these and eight other states also funded by CSP in fiscal year 1980. Originally conceived to operationalize intermediate systems change objectives by studying field operations, the study was plagued by missing-data problems which limited the scope of its findings. However, a good deal of information about program implementation as well as barriers impeding CSP accomplishments was gleaned from these field visits. As a result, the data describe basic activities that have been set in motion at the state level, and suggest some of the problems that have been encountered. Accordingly, the focus of this chapter is on implementing CSP at the state level during the program's early years.

This chapter is adapted from a document entitled "Community Support Program Performance Measurement System Development and Short-Term Evaluation Final Report." May 15, 1981, prepared by Tal Ben-Dashan, Lanny Morrison, and Martin Kotler of Macro Systems, Inc.

Focusing primarily on program implementation, this chapter also addresses some of the concerns of the plausibility analysis raised by the previous chapter. In the process of describing what state CSPs are doing, we will examine how they define the target population and its needs, how they maximize scarce programmatic and other categorical resources and access mainstream finances, and how they relate to other preexisting mental health agencies and services. In addition, this chapter describes how states are approaching mental health system change and technical assistance.

FOCAL POINT FOR COMMUNITY SUPPORT SYSTEM DEVELOPMENT

Figure 5–1 shows the state strategy development and implementation process, beginning with the establishment of a focal point for CSS development within an appropriate agency designated by the executive branch of state government. The field visits to state mental health authorities revealed that all nine of the CSP states visited have established a unit or component within the State Mental Health Agency (SMHA) which has been designated as responsible for Community Support System (CSS) development.

In each of the states, this unit was established shortly after contract award as a result of the federal CSP initiative. However, in four of the states visited, individuals responsible for assuring services to the chronically mentally ill existed prior to the CSP initiative. For example, in New Jersey, an operational/service component—Office of Community Services, within the Division of Mental Health and Hospitals—was established as early as 1975. This component continues to be responsible for the development of programs for the chronically mentally ill in the community. In the District of Columbia, the D.C. aftercare program was responsible for providing follow-up care for discharged clients and for coordinating with St. Elizabeth's Hospital. In Maine, an individual within the planning division had responsibility for the chronically mentally ill prior to the advent of CSP.

The CSP units tend to be relatively small. The average unit consists of 8.5 full-time equivalents (FTEs) for professional and support staff. However, unit size ranges from a low of 3.25 to a high of 23.75 FTEs with five of the units having 5 or fewer pro-

Figure 5-1.   Community Support Program State Strategy Development and Implementation Process Generalized Model of Field Operations.

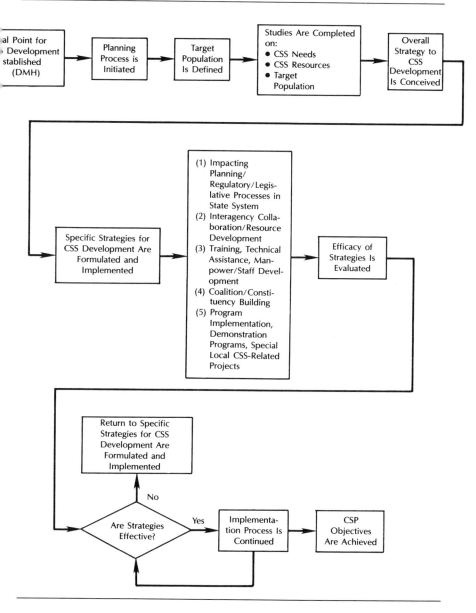

Source: Stroul, B.; L. Morrison; M. Kotler; and P. Rienzo. 1980. "Final Report of the Exploratory Evaluation of the National Institute of Mental Health Community Support Program." Appendix C:16. Silver Spring, Md.: Macro Systems, Inc.

fessional FTEs including the project director. Professional staff job titles imply an emphasis on evaluation, training, and technical assistance, substate (county, regional) coordination, planning and program development.

On the whole, support staff are supported by federal funds. In seven units, professional FTEs are supported by both state and federal CSP funds. One unit is supported by federal funds exclusively; one is funded exclusively by the state. Six of the units are headed by full-time project directors, one half of whom are state supported. The three part-time project directors are also state supported, and their time contributions to the CSP effort range from 10 to 75 percent.

DEFINITIONS OF THE TARGET POPULATION

According to the intent of the state strategy development process, an early product of state-level planning is a working definition of the target population (see Figure 5–1). Interviews conducted on site with CSP staff in state mental health agencies indicated that operational definitions of the CSP target population have been established. These definitions feature criteria in two key areas: severity of disability and functional impairment. Severity of disability criteria in the nine states visited include history of hospitalization, history of continued community-based treatment (e.g., enrollment in day treatment), maintenance on medication, residence in a transitional home, and psychiatric diagnosis. These criteria are accompanied by specifications for number, duration, and recency of treatment episodes. Criteria for impaired functioning include specifying both impaired role performance (e.g., unemployment, need for public financial assistance, inappropriate social behavior), and impaired ability to perform basic activities of daily living. Most definitions delineate the number of criteria to be met within each area.

Comparison between states in terms of their definitions of the target population show that no two definitions are completely alike. Some definitions share common criteria for either severity of disability or functional impairment. Most definitions include criteria for history of hospitalization, and most specify a similar set of criteria for impaired functioning. However, beyond these broad similarities, the definitions of the chronically mentally ill vary significantly. Key differences involve widely divergent specification in two areas related to severity of disability. These are dissimilar specification for duration, number, and time frames for hospitalization episodes, and the delineation of additional criteria for severity of disability that encompass individuals who may not have a history of hospitalization. For example, history of hospitalization criteria may specify anywhere from at least one to three hospitalizations ranging from three to six months' duration within the past six months, or within the past one, two, or five years. In addition to criteria for hospitalizations and hospital admissions, many definitions include individuals admitted or enrolled in other treatment modalities such as group homes, day care, supportive living arrangements; individuals maintained on medication for a specified period of time; individuals with a specified psychiatric diagnosis with an active case in an outpatient modality; and individuals with significant unscheduled contact with the mental health system. It should be noted that a number of states have also included restrictions against individuals who were involuntarily committed.

It is clear, given these definitional differences, that while all CSP-funded states refer to the target population as the chronically mentally ill, they may, in fact, be directing their efforts at differing populations. This finding has considerable implications not only for the comparison of activities undertaken on behalf of the chronically mentally ill across the nine CSP states visited, but also for aggregating and generalizing from study findings.

IDENTIFICATION OF CLIENT NEEDS

Based on the state's definition of its target population, CSP guidelines mandate the conducting of studies to assess the needs of potential clients and the identifying of gaps in services and resources. Results from such studies are to be used to conceptualize an overall strategy for CSS development (see Figure 5–1).

It appears that the CSP projects have identified needs for the chronically mentally ill in their states and are directing efforts, to a greater or lesser extent, to meeting such needs. Essential service needs generally have included psychosocial services (including employment), rehabilitative and supportive housing, case management, crisis assistance, assistance in meeting basic human needs, transportation, and mental health care. Table 5–1 displays the needs identified as a result of the short-term evaluation data-gathering effort. In addition, it indicates the relative priority assigned to each need at the time of the field visit interview. As inspecting these data reveals, there is little consistency in the relative priority assigned to each type of service. Of the nine states, "rehabilitative and supportive housing" was the most commonly checked first priority area.

While priorities do exist, only in a minority of the states visited were these priorities based on systematic assessment of client needs on a statewide basis. Rather, the CSP states seem to have taken an ad hoc approach to needs determination. That is, states' CSS development strategies focus on meeting needs that have generally been documented in the professional literature and which are also inherent in the ten CSS components.

While many CSS development-related activities are state-specific in terms of focus and scope, a number of general strategies typify all funded states. Information obtained both from field visits and project documents indicates that all the CSP projects have initiated an extensive array of activities aimed at establishing the chronically mentally ill as a priority population and altering policies to address their needs. These activities are consistent with CSP guidelines (see Figure 5–1). The efforts emphasize the development of interagency collaborative relationships, legislative activity, and technical assistance and training. These activities are described, in turn, in the following sections.

INTERAGENCY COLLABORATION

Interagency and collaborative activities undertaken by the CSP units in each state are numerous. True to the CSP philosophy, these collaborative efforts have not been limited to the mental health sector; they extend into the health, social services, housing, vocational rehabilitation, and transportation arenas. Almost all interagency commitments were established after the CSP contract award, and most of these have been initiated by the CSP

Table 5–1. Target Population Service Needs as Prioritized during Short-term Evaluation Field Visits

Service Needs	AZ	DC	ME[a]	MI	MN	MO	NJ[b]	SD[c]	TX
Assistance in meeting Basic Human Needs (income maintenance, benefits, entitlements, medical and dental care, etc.)	6	1	6	3	6	2	2	–	4
Mental Health Care	1	4	–	5	5	7	–	–	–
Crisis Assistance	3	5	–	2	4	6	–	2	–
Psychosocial Services	5	2	4	6	2	4	4	3	1
Rehabilitative and Supportive Housing	2	3	1	4	1	1	3	5	2
Case Management	4	1	5	1	3	3	–	4	3
Other									
Transportation	–	–	3	–	–	–	–	6	–
Employment	–	–	2	–	–	–	1	1	–

[a]This information is based on a needs assessment conducted by the Maine CSP project in 1978.
[b]This information is based on a study of a small sample of discharged clients.
[c]This information is based on needs assessments conducted in four CSP demonstration sites.

Source: Macro Systems Inc. 1981. "Community Support Program Performance Measurement System Development and Short-Term Evaluation Final Report." IV–6, Silver Spring, MD.

unit. Interagency relationships and commitments range from formal to informal arrangements. They can be characterized as follows: task forces or committees engaging multiple agencies and individuals including representatives of the CSP unit, working agreements between the CSP unit and a CSS-relevant agency, contractual agreements with a range of agencies and service providers, and ad hoc, informal meetings with a multitude of groups, organizations, and individuals.

Task forces and committees are the most common means of developing and maintaining interagency relationships and collaboration. Many of these efforts were initiated by the CSP unit for the purpose of involving and informing key individuals about the state's CSP endeavor. For example, Minnesota's CSP unit has convened an interdepartmental advisory committee which serves not only to provide direction for the CSP effort but to heighten awareness among selected state-level agencies regarding the chronically mentally ill and their needs. Maine, for example, has established a committee consisting of representatives from the state's manpower development program, the Council of Community Mental Health Centers (CMHCs), and the CSP unit to jointly sponsor and write a grant proposal for a training program for boarding home and foster home staffs and operators.

While most interagency relationships have been initiated by the CSP unit, numerous task forces and committees have been started by others. Often, these interagency groups have been formed on the initiative of an external mandate (e.g., legislation or executive order, at the SMHA level) or by another agency or program, or sponsored jointly by CSP and a relevant agency. In these instances, a CSP staff person is a representative member of either the CSP unit, the SMHA, or the umbrella agency. Membership on such bodies offers the CSP unit visibility and an opportunity to emphasize issues pertinent to CSS development. A good example is a task force established in South Dakota as a result of a directive originating at the SMHA level. This task force includes representatives from the SMHA (including CSP), the state hospital, CMHCs, Mental Health Association, and minority agencies. The purpose of this task force is to discuss, lobby, and sponsor CSS-relevant and other mental-health-related legislation.

Apart from these relatively formal mechanisms, informal ad hoc meetings with a wide range of agencies, groups, and individuals characterize a substantial proportion of the interagency relationships. Some state projects reported that these informal arrangements are often more productive than more formal task forces, committees, and contractual relationships.

While some interagency activities have not yet been fruitful, on the whole, state CSP projects report that beneficial outcomes have been realized as a result of these efforts. First, many states claim that interagency efforts have led to the modification of policies, procedures, and standards governing state and local operations, and that these changes will help to better address the needs of the chronically mentally ill. For example, in Maine the CSP unit regional coordinators worked with CMHCs to implement area mental health plans which specify the chronically mentally ill as a priority population. Second, most states report that resources (staff and funds) have been redirected on behalf of the chronically mentally ill due to interagency collaborative efforts— for example, housing slots made available as a result of collaboration with the state housing agency, services provided to the chronically mentally ill by public health nurses as a result of an informal working relationship with the Department of Health, and local agencies supplementing state funds to provide specific services to the target population.

LEGISLATIVE ACTIVITY

The legislative arena has been another important area in which CSP-funded states report a range of activities with tangible or potential impact. CSP staff are providing expert testimony at legislative hearings, and assisting in the development and writing of specific bills that concern the welfare of the chronically mental ill. Legislative activities have emphasized housing and residential issues. At least nine of the seventeen states funded in 1981 reported introducing legislation addressing zoning and other issues related to the establishment of an appropriate array of residential opportunities in the community. Other legislation introduced has focused on recipient rights and nursing home-boarding home resident rights; appropriation of funds to establish community-based services for the target population; Medicaid reimbursement for outpatients, partial care, and case management; and requirements for discharge planning for patients leaving institutions. Ten states indicated that pertinent legislation has been enacted.

A number of states had pertinent legislation in place prior to the CSP initiative. For example, New York State had prior legislation enabling the appropriation of state funds for providing community-based mental health and social services to individuals who had resided in state institutions for five or more years. In addition, New York legislatively mandated that the SMHA identify and develop treatment plans to meet the unmet needs of former mental patients who were not currently receiving services. Also prior to CSP, the state of Colorado approved the transfer of funds from state hospitals to selected community programs, and statutory authority for the funding of community-based alternatives to hospitalization was enacted in Oregon.

TECHNICAL ASSISTANCE AND TRAINING

It was clear from the field visits that CSP states provide, coordinate, or sponsor extensive technical assistance and training activities. In all funded states, technical assistance and training constitute a salient aspect of the CSS development effort. CSP projects view such activities as an important means of dissemination of information regarding the CSS philosophy and approach, gaining visibility, and developing a cadre of providers who are sensitive to the needs of the chronically mentally ill. Technical assistance efforts appear to be targeted at a broad spectrum of recipients and groups including: CMHC staff and directors; mental health and non-mental health agencies and providers at regional, county, and local levels; state level agencies; legislative committees and aides; and state hospital staff and directors. Most often training and technical assistance are provided directly or coordinated by CSP unit staff. In some cases, CSP staff participate in training efforts sponsored by other CSP projects, NIMH, and others.

Most training is provided in the form of workshops and conferences held on a statewide or substate basis. Training in a few states is also provided during site visits to service areas or programs, or through courses and symposiums. Technical assistance, on the other hand, is frequently provided directly through face-to-face contacts, presentations, or, to a lesser extent, through technical assistance materials such as manuals and newsletters.

Technical assistance and training activities are focusing on broad programmatic and conceptual issues including CSS concepts, philosophy, goals and principles; the chronically mentally ill and their needs; and development and delivery of services to the target population. Housing and case management tend to receive special emphasis, as do such CSS-relevant services as emergency care, crisis intervention, models of psychosocial services, vocational rehabiliation, and protection of client rights.

SYSTEMS CHANGE

In the area of systems change assessment, the researchers from Macro Systems, Inc., encountered a decided lack of information. This was not entirely unexpected because project reporting requirements during CSP's initial three years did not call for systematic attention to the measurement of systems change. As a result, the field visits provided only limited insight into such aspects of systems change as resource mobilization, CSS development, statewide service improvement, and the testing of CSP-relevant hypotheses linking specific activities with CSS development and service system improvement.

The area of resource mobilization illustrates some of the difficulties encountered. States did not have information on hand to indicate the extent to which resources have been mobilized on behalf of the target population. In general, states could only provide financial information on federal CSP funds expended for state-level and local CSS efforts, and state contributions to the CSP unit responsible for the target population. A number of states could provide some data on other federal resources expended such as HUD Section 202 or Title XX funds, and some state-level resources such as grants and contracts targeted for the chronically mentally ill. However, these instances were by and large estimates, and exceptions rather than the rule.

BARRIERS AND OBSTACLES

Information on barriers and obstacles which impede program performance and movement toward CSP objectives was also collected during the field visits to nine CSP-funded states. Barriers identified by the CSP projects ranged from agency-specific problems to systemwide difficulties. While many states described barriers that are specific to their systems, a number of problems common to most states also emerged. These shared problems are described below.

Most CSP states identified funding and reimbursement requirements, especially Medicaid, as a major barrier standing in the way of developing CSSs statewide. Existing funding mechanisms tend to support traditional, medical, or institutional services. Resulting gaps related to housing, transportation, sheltered workshops, case management, and transitional employment are not readily filled without special categorical support.

Most of the CSP projects visited report that public mental hospitals continue to receive the largest share of the states' mental health budget despite the flow of patients into the community. States appear to be perpetuating a dual system of care in which public hospitals compete with community programs for scarce mental health dollars. The continuation of a dual mental health system is underscored by the lack of integration and coordination between state hospitals and community-based services in many of the states visited. In South Dakota, for example, the Human Services Center (i.e., the state hospital) is administered by the Board of Charities and Corrections, a constitutionally designated body separate and autonomous from the Office of Mental Health which is responsible for the CSS. While efforts are being made to bridge the gap between hospital and community, the separation of the two systems continues to be problematic.

Attitudinal and conceptual problems were also identified. Many CSP projects observed that providers are reluctant to serve the chronically mentally ill. In some states, local human service providers continue to believe that services to the chronic patients can and should be provided by the mental health system alone. Several CSP projects discussed neighborhood resistance to community residences, negative community attitudes toward the chronically mentally ill, and a lack of community concern. Finally, there was ample indication of a general resistance to change at all levels of the service delivery system and a commitment to the status quo.

SUMMARY AND CONCLUSIONS

This chapter provides an overview of the recent CSP experience at the state level. As shown, this experience is broadly consistent with the intended process of state strategy development and implementation. CSP units are in place within state mental health agencies; working definitions of the target population have been established; clients' needs have been identified; and a variety of change strategies have been set in motion, including new interagency linkages, legislative activity, and technical training.

Missing and incomplete information limited our ability to examine CSP accomplishments in the areas of resource mobilization, CSS development, and improvements in the larger mental health delivery system. Similarly, it was not possible to use these data to test causal hypotheses concerning the link between specific activities at the state level and improvements in statewide services. The absence of evidence for such a link remains as a significant threat to program plausibility. Nonetheless, the data are informative, and considerable insight is provided about the barriers encountered in implementing CSP at the state level.

In the next two chapters we shift our focus to the local level. Chapter 6 describes the characteristics of clients in the local demonstration sites and their actual use of support services, and Chapter 7 examines factors affecting clients' adjustment to community living.

THE CLIENTS

6 CLIENT PROFILE AND USE OF SERVICES

Community support programs (CSPs) have emerged as a new conceptual model to improve the quality of life of the chronically mentally ill in community settings. As adapted by the National Institute of Mental Health (NIMH) CSP, the model specified ten essential components for comprehensive care (Turner and TenHoor 1978; Turner and Shifren 1979). These ten components extended beyond the boundaries of the mental health system and required coordination with other health and human service agencies. At the state level, a special CSP unit was to be established which would assess the needs of the target population and lobby for the state-wide interests of the chronically mentally ill. At the local level, a core service agency was to be designated which would take responsibility for securing and integrating all ten service components in order to create a genuine community support system (CSS). At the client level, a case manager (an individual or team) was to remain in contact with the client on a continuing basis in order to assure that each client was receiving appropriate services.

This chapter reports the descriptive findings from a national survey conducted in 1980 by the NIMH of CSP clients and their use of services in eighteen different sites. The chapter serves two purposes. One purpose is to illustrate a viable research instrument and methodology for gathering client-level data which can be adapted for use at the state and local levels. The second purpose is to report some substantive findings from this NIMH survey, and in so doing to describe the characteristics of the chronically mentally ill in CSSs around the country, as well as the scope of services currently being provided.

While the descriptive data should not be generalized too widely because of the special nature of this client population, it does provide a "snapshot" of one group of chronically mentally ill persons who are trying to cope with the many challenges of community (rather than institutional) life. Accordingly, the present chapter describes the clients' entry into the program, their demographic characteristics, clinical histories, and some indicators of their current functioning. In an effort to assess how comprehensively clients are being served, we also examine utilization data corresponding to the ten essential components of a CSS.

METHODS

Data were collected using the Uniform Client Data Instrument (UCDI) developed by NIMH for use in the evaluation of CSP. Each case manager provided a list of client numbers and, from among these, the research staff selected a random sample of clients for inclusion in the study. A total of 248 case managers participated. On the average, each case manager provided data on seven clients. Table 6–1 shows the number and proportion of clients sampled out of the total number of clients in each site, and the number of participating case managers at each site. This list of sites includes three "replication" sites in addition to the original fifteen funded demonstration sites located in twelve states.

As Table 6–1 shows, UCDIs were completed for 1,471 clients, or 34.3 percent of the estimated 4,288 persons participating in this program. To derive estimates for the federal program, these data were weighted by a sampling fraction based on the number of clients served at each site divided by the number of UCDIs which were actually completed. In examining the results, it is important to remember that the numbers describing CSP clients constitute projections based on the assumption that the sampled cases were representative of the total client population.

Two visits were made to each site in early 1980 in order to acquaint the case managers with the data-collection plans and to familiarize local staff with the questionnaire (that is, the UCDI). Based on the initial visit we assessed the feasibility of the approach and also made some changes in the questionnaire. One to two months intervened between the first and second visits. In the actual study, case managers were encouraged to consult existing records and other staff members as necessary in order to complete the UCDIs. Procedures were also established to ensure the anonymity of the client data. Data collection commenced in the spring of 1980, or soon after the second field visit by a representative of the research team. Most sites were able to mail in the completed UCDIs within three to four weeks. Each UCDI required a median time of forty-two minutes to complete.

The UCDI included the following types of data elements:

Table 6–1. Total Number of CSP Clients Served, Number of Clients Sampled, Number of Case Managers Sampled, and Percent CSP Clients Sampled at Each Site.

Site	Number of Clients Sampled out of Total Number of CSP Clients	Percent CSP Clients Sampled	Number of Participating Case Managers
Redding, California	30/137	22	3
Santa Rosa, California	57/260	22	6
Denver, Colorado	60/200	30	7
Miami, Florida	143/310	46	16
Schenectady, New York	52/350	15	16
Syracuse, New York	54/400	14	11
Wingdale, New York	115/500	23	30
Brockton, Massachusetts	119/560	21	34
Ann Arbor, Michigan	92/209	44	34
St. Louis, Missouri	115/144	94	7
Minneapolis, Minnesota	116/352	33	13
Billings, Montana	146/229	64	30
Huron, South Dakota	46/60	77	7
Mitchell, South Dakota	20/67	30	2
Yankton, South Dakota	63/143	44	10
Dallas, Texas	48/83	58	8
Wichita Falls, Texas	44/75	59	1
Washington, D.C.	151/209	72	13
TOTAL	1471/4288		248

1. *Entry* information including: source of referral to CSP, length of time in the program, and the case manager's familiarity with the client (date of first contact and most recent contact, four-point rating scale of familiarity).
2. *Demographic* information including: age, sex, race, marital status, education, employment status, monthly income and sources, housing, and family involvement.
3. *Clinical history* information including: age at first psychiatric admission, number of times hospitalized, length of stay in psychiatric facilities, and psychiatric diagnosis.
4. *Current functioning* information including: measures of somatic problems, basic living skills, social activities, behavioral problems, victimization by others, and global ratings of disability and social adjustment.
5. *Service utilization* information including: the types of community support services provided to clients in a one-month period in the basic areas of client need as defined by the ten essential CSS components.

DESCRIPTIVE FINDINGS

Entry Information

Two questions in the UCDI concerned how clients entered CSP and the length of time they had been in the program. In terms of the source of clients' most recent referral to CSP, the results showed that the majority of clients were referred by publicly supported institutions. The most frequent source (34.8%) was from public psychiatric hospitals where the client had been an inpatient. The other most frequently checked sources were Community Mental Health Centers (13.5%), Outpatient Public Mental Health facilities (12.0%), and other Human Service Agencies (11.4%). In relatively few cases was the client self-referred (5.2%), or referred by relatives (4.1%), clergy (1.0%), roommates (1.0%), or private practitioners (1.0%). It is also noteworthy that "outreach case finding" was checked in only 0.2 percent of the cases. The small number of cases resulting from outreach efforts (9 out of 4256), as well as the small number of referrals from nontraditional sources (clergy, counselors, housemates, etc.) indicate that few outreach efforts have gone beyond the established mental health system. This interpretation is further supported by responses to another question in the UCDI that revealed that 44.2 percent of the clients had been referred by the program's own local core service agency.

The case managers reported that they had managed the clients for a median time period of 10.13 (mean = 14.93) months. Case managers report knowing the client very well in 31.6 percent of the cases, moderately well in 43.2 percent of the cases, slightly in 22.3 percent of the cases, and not at all in only 2.9 percent of the cases.

Demographic Information

The median age of CSP clients is 41.80 years. Approximately 12 percent are less than twenty-four years of age and about 12 percent are 65 years of age or older. The sex distribution is 47.0 percent male and 53.0 percent female, revealing a slight preponderance of females when compared to the general U.S. population. Analysis of the racial composition shows a predominantly white group (89.1%).

As is so often found in surveys of the chronically mentally ill, only a small proportion (10.9%) is married or living in a conjugal state (1.1%). The majority have never been married (56%), or are divorced (20.9%), widowed (6.2%) or separated (4.8%).

Almost 33 percent of these clients are high school graduates, and a significant proportion (19.3%) have at least some college education. Nonetheless, only 25.9 percent of the clients were employed at the time of the survey. This is almost identical to the 25 percent employment figure reported in similar studies of discharged patients (Minkoff 1978; Anthony et al. 1972). Of the 25.9 percent who were working, only 41.8 percent were employed on the open market; most of these jobs involved menial work and many of these persons were only working part time. The rest of the "employed" were working in sheltered workshops (37.1%), in paid transitional employment programs (11.2%), in unpaid work training programs (8.7%), or as volunteers (1.2%).

The median estimated monthly income was $325.07, or a yearly income of about $3,900. Though we have limited confidence in the reliability of the income data, there is no doubt that this is a poor client population. According to case-manager reports, 47.7 percent of the clients are receiving Supplemental Security Income (SSI), one third (34.9%) receive social security or Social Security Disability Income (SSDI) payments, and one fifth receive social service benefits (22.1%)

Table 6–2 shows the way in which CSP clients are distributed across a variety of housing arrangements. As these data show, over one half (55.2%) of the clients live in settings which provide little or no supervision: private homes, apartments, rooming houses, boarding houses, or unsupervised cooperative apartments. However, relatively few clients live alone (14.8%). The percent of patients living with family members (31.8%) is slightly higher than the 26 percent finding in a five-year follow-up of discharged chronic patients in California (Lamb and Goertzel 1972).

Table 6–2.   Clients' Current Housing Arrangement.

Dwelling Type	Percent
Inpatient of a psychiatric hospital or facility	4.8
Skilled nursing facility—24-hour nursing	3.5
Intermediate care facility—less than 24-hour care	0.4
Supervised group living (long term)	6.2
Transitional group home (halfway or quarterway house)	3.4
Family or foster care	10.3
Cooperative apartment, supervised (live-in or non-live-in)	3.7
Cooperative apartment, unsupervised (no continuous staff)	7.8
Board and care home (PPHA, Adults Home, with program supervision)	12.6
Boarding house (includes meals, no program or supervision)	4.7
Rooming or boarding house or hotel (SRO, no meals)	2.3
Private house or apartment	40.4
Don't know	(69)
No answer	(14)
BASE[a]	(4205)

[a]Base excludes don't knows and no answers. Numbers in parentheses are frequencies. Percents are calculated only for the remaining categories.

In order to assess the extent of clients' family involvement, case managers were asked to check whether the client has family living nearby (within one hour of driving time), and if so, whether the family is involved with the client. Responses to this question show that 67.0 percent of the clients are living within one hour's drive of a family member who is involved with the client. Only 10.0 percent of the clients had nearby family members with whom they were uninvolved.

Clinical History

The median age at which clients had their first contact for psychiatric care was 24.04 (mean = 27.37) years. The vast majority of the clients (92.3%) have been hospitalized for psychiatric care at some time in their lives, with a median total of 3.14 (mean = 4.30) admissions for each client. The clients' median age at first hospitalization was 24.84 (mean = 28.03) years. Clients have spent a median total of 22.50 months in hospitals for psychiatric illnesses. The mean average (88.80 months) was considerably higher because of the large proportion of clients (27.5%) who have spent a total of over ten years in institutions. Slightly more than one third (36.0%) of clients had been hospitalized during the past five years.

While a majority of the clients had not been hospitalized at all during the previous year, those who were hospitalized (nearly 1 in 3) spent a median of 5.9 (mean = 12.99) weeks in hospitals for psychiatric illness during that period. These figures are similar to readmission data collected on chronic client samples in previous studies (Rosenblatt and Mayer 1974). During the clients' most recent episode of hospitalization, 65.7 percent were voluntary admissions, 31.7 percent were involuntary civil admissions, and 2.7 percent were involuntary criminal admissions.

Table 6–3 shows the distribution of primary and secondary psychiatric diagnoses in this sample. Most of these diagnoses were assigned fairly recently, with 1978 recorded as the median year. As this table shows, the preponderant diagnostic categories are schizophrenia and depression. It is noteworthy that the distribution of primary diagnoses among CSP clients differs from a distribution recorded in an unpublished NIMH report on the resident

Table 6–3.   Primary and Secondary Psychiatric Diagnosis of Clients.

Diagnosis	Diagnosis	
	Primary (%)	Secondary (%)
Alcohol disorder	1.8	14.4
Drug abuse	0.2	6.5
Mental retardation	3.8	10.6
Depressive and affective disorder	12.1	17.9
Schizophrenia	68.9	5.2
Organic brain syndromes excluding alcohol and drugs	4.6	14.1
Other psychoses	1.3	4.0
Other nonpsychotic mental disorders	6.6	13.8
Social maladjustment	0.8	14.0
Don't know	(99)	(272)
No answer	(69)	(3117)
BASE[a]	(4119)	(899)

[a]Base excludes don't knows and no answers. Numbers in parentheses are frequencies. Percents are calculated only for the remaining categories.

population in U.S. state and county mental hospitals in 1979. Compared with the 1979 resident population, the CSP population has a higher percentage of diagnosed schizophrenia (69% versus 52%) and depressive disorders (12% versus 6%), and lower proportions of mental retardation (4% versus 8%), organic brain syndromes (5% versus 18%), and alcohol disorders (2% versus 5%). According to case manager reports at the time of the study, psychotropic medications were being prescribed to control the symptoms and behavior of 84.4 percent of the CSP clients.

Current Functioning

The results for this section of the UCDI are divided into six subsections: somatic problems, basic living skills, social activities, behavioral problems, victimization, and global ratings. Each of these is discussed below.

Somatic Problems.   In order to comprehensively serve the chronically mentally ill, it is important to take account of their physical health problems, especially as these problems affect their ability to function independently. One set of items in the UCDI focused specifically on this issue. Case managers were asked whether clients had any chronic medical problems that interfere with their daily activities or functioning. Based on the data provided by the case managers, it was projected that more than four of every ten clients (44.7%) experience some interference due to one or more problems affecting their physical health. Among clients experiencing some interference, the most common problems reported were obesity/undernourishment (27.4%), medication side effects (21.8%), impaired motor control (20.4%), and circulatory and heart disorders (18.1%). In the next chapter, we will demonstrate that, among clients who work, the presence of somatic problems is a significant predictor of work performance, as indicated by type of job, number of hours per week, and earned income.

Basic Living Skills.   Successful community adjustment demands a varied repertoire of skills and abilities, and where clients' repertoires are deficient in important areas, special attention may be required. Table 6–4 contains the case managers' estimates of their clients' skills in relation to some basic requirements of successful community living. For each basic living skill, case managers indicated the client's degree of independence and, regardless of assistance, whether he or she was unable or unwilling to act independently.

Examination of Table 6–4 shows that about nine out of ten of the clients are totally independent in terms of their ability to dress themselves and to walk and get around. With minor assistance or supervision, most of the clients are also able to maintain adequate diet (80.3%), perform household chores (80.4%), go shopping (80.2%), use available transportation on familiar routes (78.7%), and maintain personal hygiene (89.7%). The basic skill areas in which clients have the most difficulty and need the most assistance are in verbalizing their needs and in securing necessary

Table 6–4. Degree to which Clients Perform Basic Living Skills Independently.

Basic Living Skill	Acts Independently	Needs Minor Assistance or Supervision	Has Difficulty and Needs Assistance	Unable To Act Independently	Unwilling To Act Independently	BASE[a]
				Degree of Independence		
Maintains personal hygiene	68.6	21.1	7.6	0.7	2.0	(4185)
Dresses self	89.0	7.8	2.4	0.5	0.2	(4199)
Walks/Gets around	92.8	4.2	1.8	0.7	0.6	(4155)
Maintains adequate diet	55.1	25.2	11.1	5.6	3.0	(3805)
Prepares/Obtains own meals	57.8	18.3	10.9	8.9	4.0	(3175)
Maintains prescribed program of medication	45.1	28.0	14.5	6.9	5.5	(3688)
Performs household chores	58.5	21.9	8.4	5.7	5.5	(3452)
Goes shopping	60.4	19.8	9.6	7.0	3.2	(3838)
Uses available transportation on familiar routes	69.5	9.2	4.6	12.6	4.0	(3905)
Uses available transportation on unfamiliar routes	47.5	21.0	9.9	15.9	5.9	(3649)
Manages available funds	48.4	24.0	14.1	11.9	1.6	(4015)
Secures necessary support services	37.6	31.5	17.4	9.3	4.1	(4054)
Is able to verbalize needs	51.4	23.5	19.4	4.2	1.5	(4169)

[a]Base excludes does not apply, don't knows, and no answers.

support services, maintaining prescribed programs of medication, using transportation on unfamiliar routes, preparing and obtaining meals, and managing available funds. In these areas, at least one in five clients needed some type of assistance. These results document the continuing need for training in selected basic living skills, and the importance of assuring that supportive services are available on a 24-hour basis for some clients.

Social Activities.   Because a majority of the CSP clients (74.1%) are not working in any capacity, many encounter a problem in finding things to do with their time each day. Clients' degree of engagement in daily social activities, including both working and nonworking clients, is shown in Table 6–5. Inspection of these data indicates that, for a significant minority of clients, social and leisure time is not productively filled. For example, 16.9 percent of the clients never engage in any scheduled daytime activity, and almost one quarter (23.5%) do so only once a week or less. Almost 12 percent never socialize with friends, and 30.2 percent do so no more than once a week. Large proportions never or only infrequently engage in recreational activities outside the home.

While these socialization figures appear low, they actually reflect a higher level of friendship and social activity than other studies of the chronically mentally ill (Davis, Dinitz, and Pasamanick 1974; Freeman and Simmons 1963; Myers and Bean 1964; Sanders, Smith, and Weinman 1967; Lamb and Goertzel 1977; Brown et al. 1966). It is tempting to infer that CSP clients are more socially active by virtue of their participation in CSSs, but such a conclusion would be premature at this time.

Behavioral Problems.   Table 6–6 shows the list of behavioral problems included in the UCDI, along with the case managers' ratings of the presence and seriousness of these problems for individual clients. For seven of the fifteen behaviors listed, about 90 percent or more of the clients were reported to have no problem at all. These include the following percentages of clients reported to have no problem: incontinence (93.7%); engaged in inappropriate sexual behavior (91.4%); had trouble with the law (92.7%); destroyed or stole property (93.8%); abused drugs (90.8%); made suicidal threats or attempts (88.9%); used matches, cigarettes, or fire hazardously (92.3%). These data suggest a fairly low frequen-

Table 6–5. Frequency of Clients' Participation in Social Activities.

Social Activity	Never (%)	Frequency Once a Week or Less (%)	2-3 Days a Week (%)	4-5 Days a Week (%)	6-7 Days a Week (%)	BASE[a]
Socializes with family members	19.9	45.5	10.7	5.2	18.8	(3536)
Socializes with friends	11.7	30.2	22.4	12.3	23.5	(3590)
Engages in any scheduled daytime activity	16.9	23.5	19.5	28.6	11.5	(3683)
Engages in recreational activities at home, other than TV or radio	25.6	37.0	20.1	8.0	9.2	(3303)
Engages *alone* in recreational activities outside the home (e.g., movies, sports, lectures, visits parks)	48.7	34.6	10.8	2.6	3.4	(3293)
Engages *with others* in recreational activities outside the home (e.g., movies, sports, lectures, visits parks)	26.1	45.7	20.3	4.9	3.0	(3511)
Attends clubs, lodge or other meetings	67.9	21.6	6.7	2.7	1.1	(3227)
Goes to church or other religious services	54.2	40.6	4.1	0.2	0.9	(2806)

[a]Base excludes does not apply, don't knows, and no answers.

| | Degree of Problem | | | | |
Behavioral Problem	No Problem (%)	Minor Problem (%)	Moderate Problem (%)	Serious Problem (%)	BASE[a]
Was incontinent	93.7	4.2	1.7	0.4	(4058)
Wandered/Loitered	85.7	8.2	4.5	1.7	(4071)
Had trouble at work or school	76.0	9.8	7.7	6.5	(3481)
Caused complaints from household	66.2	15.4	11.3	7.1	(3906)
Caused community complaints	84.8	7.2	3.8	4.1	(3914)
Engaged in inappropriate sexual behavior	91.4	4.3	2.6	1.7	(3910)
Exhibited temper tantrums	80.6	9.2	6.2	4.0	(3980)
Had trouble with the law	92.7	3.1	2.6	1.5	(3999)
Destroyed/Stole property	93.8	2.2	1.6	2.4	(3995)
Abused alcohol	86.8	5.9	4.2	3.2	(3926)
Abused drugs (includes legal, illegal, prescribed and nonprescription drugs)	90.8	4.0	2.8	2.4	(3924)
Made violent threats or attempts	86.9	4.7	4.1	4.3	(2771)[b]
Made suicidal threats or attempts	88.9	5.8	2.8	2.6	(3985)
Engaged in bizarre behavior	74.7	12.8	8.0	4.5	(4031)
Used matches, cigarettes, or fire hazardously	92.3	4.9	1.2	1.5	(3981)

[a]Base excludes don't knows, no answers, and not applicable.
[b]This base is reduced because the New York State sites did not provide ratings on this behavior problem.

cy of occurrence for many behaviors that the community would view as disruptive or threatening. They contrast with community beliefs about the chronically mentally ill.

Those behaviors for which more than 10 percent of the clients are rated as having moderate or serious problems are: had trouble at work or school (14.2%); caused complaints from household (18.4%); exhibited temper tantrums (10.2%); and engaged in bizarre behavior (12.5%). Finally, three behaviors were rated as posing moderate or serious problems in 5 to 10 percent of the clients. These are: wandered/loitered (6.2%); caused community complaints (7.9%); and abused alcohol (7.4%).

Victimization. Popular beliefs about the chronically mentally ill tend to highlight instances of bizarre behavior and its disruptiveness for community life. Proportionately less attention is given to the client as a victim of life in the community. In order to shift this emphasis, we included some items in the UCDI to assess the frequency with which clients are victims of violent crimes (such as assault, mugging, robbery, or rape) and property crimes (such as burglary, larceny, cheating, swindles, or confidence tricks). Combining the figures for violent and property crimes reveals that 2.5 percent (unduplicated count) had been victimized at least once during the prior month, and that 6.2 percent (unduplicated count) had been crime victims during the prior six months. While these data indicate that victimization is a relatively rare event in this population, the absolute numbers of clients afflicted by these crimes are certainly not trivial. Due to lack of full information, the case manager reports may also underestimate the true prevalence of violent and property crime afflicted upon this vulnerable population. In any case, these victimization rates are higher than victimization rates in the general population as reported by the National Crime Survey (Law Enforcement Assistance Administration 1979).

Global Ratings. When asked to rate how mentally disabled the clients had been in the past month in comparison to the community in general, the case managers rated 17.1 percent as severely disabled and 43.2 percent as moderately disabled. Case managers also provided global ratings of clients' social adjustment at work, school, or training; at home or residence; and in leisure activities.

In general, these adjustment ratings were more positive than the global rating of mental disability. Only about 20 to 30 percent of the clients were rated as being severely or poorly adjusted in any of these three areas. Clients received the most positive ratings of social adjustment "at home or residence," where only 5.0 percent were rated as severely maladjusted and only 14.6 percent were rated as poorly adjusted.

Service Utilization

The present section focuses on the utilization of services by CSP clients. Analysis of utilization data is important because these data indicate whether, and to what extent, CSP clients are being comprehensively served. Are essential components of CSP being translated into specific services for the chronically mentally ill? In order to assess patterns of use, case managers were presented with a list of services pertinent to CSP's ten essential components. For each item, the case manager indicated if the service was used by the client during the past month and if the case manager was involved in securing or coordinating the service.[1]

1. The first guiding principle for a CSS is that it locate chronically mentally ill persons and assure their access to needed services and community resources by arranging for transportation, if necessary, or by taking the services to the clients. Since this survey focused only on clients who were already involved in CSSs, the utilization data do not provide any additional insight about people who should be in the system and who are not. However, data pertinent to assistance in securing transportation for clients who are currently in the system are available. During the one-month period under study, a vehicle was provided for about 30 percent of the clients and, for about 16 percent of clients, a transportation subsidy was secured.

2. The second guiding principle is to help CSS clients meet basic human needs for food, clothing, shelter, personal safety, general medical and dental care, and to assist them in applying for income, medical, housing and other benefits which they may need and to which they are entitled. According to case managers' reports, about 40 percent of the clients received medical care during the previous month, and 8.7 percent received dental care during

the same period. Approximately 20 percent of the clients in the month under study had their benefit status assessed and/or were directly assisted in applying for income, medical, and other entitlements. About 20 percent of the clients were referred during the month under study to appropriate community resources to secure entitlement benefits.

3. The third service principle is to provide: adequate mental health care, including diagnostic evaluation; prescription, periodic review and regulation of psychotropic drugs as needed; and community-based psychiatric, psychological or counseling and treatment services. The UCDI item which is most pertinent to the above concerned noncrisis outpatient mental health services. Almost 60 percent of the clients received this service in the past month, according to case managers' reports. Unfortunately, additional information about the content of these outpatient services is not available.

4. The fourth service principle is to provide 24-hour, quick-response crisis assistance directed toward maintaining the client's status as a functioning community member to the greatest extent possible. This function is best indicated by two items in the UCDI: emergency client contact and emergency hospitalization. Based on the information provided by the case managers, it appears that about one in six clients received an emergency client contact in the prior month. About one of every thirteen clients received an emergency hospitalization.

5. This next principle is to provide comprehensive psychosocial services including, but not limited to: helping clients evaluate their strengths and weaknesses; training clients in daily and community-living skills; helping clients develop social skills, interests and leisure time activities; and helping clients find and make use of appropriate employment opportunities. According to the UCDI data, about one half of the clients received an assessment of their psychosocial needs during the prior month (52.0%). Almost one quarter participated in activities focusing on community living skills (23.5%). Recreational and socialization activities were also provided to many of the clients during the past month, including planned daytime activities (50.2%), planned evening activities (33.3%), and planned weekend and holiday activities (29.4%). While such services were provided to large numbers of clients, it is important to note that the time

frame employed was an entire month, and numerous inactive days and weeks probably intervened for many of these clients. Some clients were also engaged in activities designed to enhance employability including prevocational rehabilitation (17.9%), vocational counseling and training (17.9%), and sheltered workshops (11.1%).

6. To be fully comprehensive, a CSS must also assure that a range of special housing options and living arrangements are available for clients who are not in a state of crisis. These options should be made available for an indefinite duration. Analysis of the UCDI data shows that during the prior month 12.4 percent of the clients were assisted to locate appropriate housing.

7. The next principle calls attention to the need to offer backup support, assistance, and consultation and education to families, friends, landlords, employers, community agencies and others who are in frequent contact with CSP clients. For the one month under study, the data from the UCDI show that, for 49.2 percent of the clients, case managers had contact with significant others (family, friends, and other community members). In addition, supportive assistance and consultation was provided to 28.2 percent of families, friends, and community members by persons other than the case manager.

8. According to CSP guidelines, it is imperative that mental health professionals recognize the potential role of natural support systems (neighborhood networks, churches, community organizations, commerce and industry) and work with these groups to increase opportunities for mentally disabled persons to participate in community life. There is some evidence that CSP staff are reaching out to involve concerned community members. According to the UCDI data, concerned community members were involved during the prior month for 15.6 percent of clients in activities related to housing, and for 10.3 percent of the clients in activities related to employment.

9. A ninth principle is to establish grievance procedures and mechanisms to protect client rights, both in and outside of mental health or residential facilities. In response to three pertinent questions in the UCDI, case managers indicated that during the past month 19.1 percent of the clients had been informed of rights and grievance procedures, 10 percent received training in

legal rights, and in 8.3 percent of the cases some type of advocacy occurred concerning grievance or legal procedures.

10. A final principle concerns the importance of designating an individual or team as responsible for each client. This function is often referred to as case management. Consistent with this principle, each of the clients in the study had a case manager, though other job titles were often used. Data from the utilization section of the UCDI show that 46.28 percent of the clients received face-to-face contact with the case manager during the prior month, and that case managers contacted 35.39 percent of the clients by telephone. It is also important to note that, where specific services were received by clients in the month under study, the case managers were involved in securing or coordinating the vast majority of these services. For example, where clients received assistance in locating housing during the prior month, the case managers were involved over 86 percent of the time.

Effects of Client Characteristics on Services Utilization

In order to inquire whether utilization of community support services was randomly distributed in this client population, we computed a summary index of utilization, based on the items described in the preceding section ($\overline{X}$ = 8.12, S.D. = 4.32), and used multiple regression to relate this index to three measures of client need and two measures of community adjustment.[2] To the extent that utilization was focused on the "neediest" clients, we reasoned that the analysis would show significant effects due to client need. Three measures of client need were included in the analysis. One was an index of basic living skills, representing the number of areas in which clients experience problems in everyday living, weighted by the mean severity of these problems. A second index was composed of behavioral problems, and also employed a problem count weighted by a mean severity score. The third index was a simple count of the number of chronic somatic problems present that could impair or restrict independent activity.

In addition, we regressed the index of services utilization on two measures of community adjustment. One was a measure of social activity, reflecting the clients' involvement in social and recreational activities. The second was a measure of work status, which showed whether the client was working and if he or she was earning income. As with the client need variables, we anticipated that the more poorly adjusted clients would be using the most services.

The results are presented in Table 6–7. They show that two of the three client-need variables (behavioral problems and basic living skills) were related in the expected direction to utilization, but fail to show a significant relationship between somatic problems and receipt of services.[3] Surprisingly, the strongest predictor of utilization was social and recreational activity which showed that utilization was highest among the more active clients. While the direction of this relationship was unexpected, in hindsight it seems likely that social and recreational activity was itself an indicator of services utilization, and that the two measures were confounded. Utilization was also higher among persons who were not gainfully employed, as predicted, but the effect was very modest. The multiple regression equation, including client need and adjustment variables, accounted for a total of 8.18 percent of the variance in utilization.

Reasoning that some of these findings may actually be due to differences between the eighteen CSSs under study rather than to client characteristics, we also recomputed the regression equation so as to include dummy variables representing the different CSSs (data not shown). When these dummy variables are entered alone

Table 6–7. Regression of Utilization on Measures of Client Need and Adjustment (N = 1471).[a]

Independent Variable	Standardized Regression Coefficient
Living Skills	.13[b]
Somatic Problems	−.01
Behavioral Problems	.11[b]
Social Activities	.22[b]
Work Status	.10[b]

Note: R^2 = .082
[a]See Note 2 of this chapter
[b]$p < .001$

in the regression equation, they account for 11.4 percent of the variance in utilization. Addition of the three indicators of client need and the two adjustment variables replicated the results of the initial analysis, and further increased the R^2 to 18.1 percent. Clearly, the site effects were largely independent of the client need and adjustment variables, suggesting that relations between client characteristics and services utilization are not mere artifacts of selection biases in the recruitment of clients at different sites.

DISCUSSION

A major purpose of this study was to assess the feasibility of a methodology which depends on case managers to provide client descriptive data and to pilot test the UCDI. The results indicate that it is feasible to ask case managers to answer most, if not all, of the questions in the UCDI. Each questionnaire required a median time of forty-two minutes to complete. The most time-consuming section of the UCDI was the clinical history section. Case managers often consulted existing records and other staff menbers in order to provide these data. The clinical history section also elicited the greatest number of "don't know" responses, but for most of the items in this and other sections of the instrument the proportion of "don't know" responses was within generally acceptable limits. Those questions which were most difficult for case managers to answer were: total monthly income, frequency and duration of hospitalizations, secondary diagnosis, and certain of the social activity items.[4]

It is difficult to assess whether the level of service utilization within any given component was appropriate or not. The utilization items focused only on the one-month period prior to the study, and clients who did not receive a service may not have needed the service during so brief a period of time. Future research might employ a longer time frame and note the reason a service was not delivered; that is, the service may have been offered and refused, the service may not have been offered because of a lack of appropriate resources, or there simply may have been no need for the service.

It was not feasible to check on the accuracy of the entry, demographic, clinical history, and utilization data. However, these items did not require that the case managers make subjective judgments. Where subjectivity was a factor, in the current functioning section, we did try to assess inter-rater reliability based on a subsample of cases for which two independent ratings could be obtained. While the results of this study of inter-rater reliability were encouraging, especially in those cases where both raters knew the client "very well," they were not conclusive and further research is needed.[5]

The methodology and instrument can be further refined and adapted to other settings. It is possible, on the basis of the national field test of the instrument, to develop a short form of the UCDI which would reduce the burden on respondents. Ideally, the UCDI would be used both to provide a cross-sectional snapshot of clients' needs and their use of services and to monitor changes in client functioning and utilization by collecting data about the same individuals at two or more points in time. Such a longitudinal study, based on a sample of CSSs, is currently planned by the NIMH.

Summary Profile

This chapter concludes with a summary profile of the clients. The survey results provide a national snapshot of a group of severely disabled persons who are trying to cope with life outside of institutions. The CSP clients are largely white and middle-aged, with a slight predominance of females. Few of them are employed in competitive jobs. Most of the clients are unmarried, and they live in a range of residential settings varying greatly in the incentives they provide and in their restrictiveness. Nearly one out of three clients lives with family members.

Approximately nine out of ten clients have a history of hospitalization, and over a quarter have spent ten or more years in psychiatric hospitals. Most clients were referred to CSP by publicly supported psychiatric institutions, most commonly by state mental hospitals. About two out of three clients have been assigned a primary diagnosis of schizophrenia. In addition to their psychiatric problems, many of the clients suffer from chronic medical conditions. The most common of these conditions are obesity/undernourishment, medication side effects, and impaired motor control.

The most problematic skill areas for these clients are transportation (especially on unfamiliar routes), managing money, adhering to prescribed medication regimens, preparing and obtaining meals, and verbalizing their needs and securing appropriate support services.

Many of the clients appear to lead very lonely lives. Approximately 17 percent of these clients have few or no regularly scheduled daytime activities. Nearly 12 percent are reported to have no friends whom they see each week, and more than one in four engage in no regular recreational activities outside the home. Without appropriate encouragement and support, social "vegetation" can occur as readily in the community as it does in institutions.

Contrary to many popular conceptions, the vast majority of CSP clients do not have behavioral problems that threaten or violate important social norms and widely shared expectations. It was rare to detect instances of clients wandering or loitering, engaging in inappropriate sexual behavior, destroying or stealing property, or using matches, cigarettes, or fire hazardously. Finally, a small but significant minority of the clients were recent victims of crimes against property or person.

A major section of the UCDI dealt with clients' utilization of community support services, and with the role of the case managers in securing or coordinating these services. The results show that each of the ten essential components is active, though there was much variation in use of services from site to site. For most services received by CSP clients, the case manager was involved in some way at least eighty percent of the time. Analysis of a multivariate model for the prediction of utilization revealed modest relationships between client characteristics and use of services across the ten service components. Observed relationships between indicators of client need and the receipt of services in the prior month showed, as predicted, that a greater number of services were received by clients with significant behavioral problems and deficits in basic living skills. It is reasonably clear from these data that CSSs are providing a comprehensive range of services to an appropriate target population.

NOTES

1. In addition to completing the UCDI, 211 of the 248 case managers also responded to a background questionnaire. This questionnaire included questions on the case manager's demographic characteristics, educational background, in-service training, current job activities, caseload, and relevant work history. A description of the case managers in terms of these and other pertinent variables is available in a recent dissertation by Alice Bernstein (1981). This dissertation also examines relationships between case manager background characteristics, clients' characteristics, and clients' use of community support services.

2. Whereas prior analyses have focused on the description of population parameters, the present analyses involve tests of relationships between variables. Since tests of statistical significance require generalization from a sample to a larger population, these analyses are based on the sample of 1,471 actual cases, appropriately weighted to reflect their representation in the total population of 4,288 CSP clients. For further details about this weighting procedure, as well as the construction of the five indices of client characteristics used in this section, see Chapter 7.

3. However, when the medical care item is isolated from the utilization index and itself regressed against the three independent variables, the results show a significant relationship between somatic problems and medical care utilization (Beta = .12). The index of basic living skills is also significantly related to medical care (Beta = .17).

4. An item-by-item analysis of the UCDI appears in Appendix C of the Final Report by Bernstein, Love, and Davis, entitled "Collaborative Data Collection and Analysis for Community Support Program Demonstration Projects" (1981).

5. These analyses can be found in the Final Report by Bernstein, Love, and Davis (1981); see chapter 4, pp. 3–12.

REFERENCES

Anthony, W. A.; G. J. Buell; S. Sharratt; and M. E. Althoff. 1972. "Efficacy of Psychiatric Rehabilitation." *Psychological Bulletin* 78, no. 6 (December): 447–56.

Bernstein, A. G. 1981. "Case Managers: Who Are They and Are They Making Any Difference in Mental Health Service Delivery?" Ph.D dissertation, University of Georgia.

Bernstein, A. G.; R. Love; and G. E. Davis. 1981. "Collaborative Data Collection and Analysis for Community Support Program Demonstration Projects." NIMH-Contract No. 79-0031 (OP). Rockville, Md.: National Institute of Mental Health.

Brown, G. W.; M. Bone; and B. Dalison. 1966. *Schizophrenia and Social Care.* London: Oxford University Press.

Davis, A. E.; S Dinitz; and B. Pasamanick. 1974. *Schizophrenics in the New Custodial Community: Five Years after the Experiment.* Columbus, Ohio: Ohio State University.

Freeman, H. E., and O. Simmons. 1963. *The Mental Patient Comes Home.* New York: Wiley.

Lamb, H. R., and V. Goertzel. 1972. "The Demise of the State Hospital—A Premature Obituary?" *Archives of General Psychiatry* 26, no. 6 (June): 489–95.

――――. 1977. "The Long-term Patient in the Era of Community Treatment." *Archives of General Psychiatry* 34, no. 6 (June): 679–82.

Law Enforcement Assistance Administration. 1979. Criminal Victimization in the United States 1977: A National Crime Survey Report. No. 027-000-00891-7. Washington D.C.: Government Printing Office.

Minkoff, K. 1978. "A Map of the Chronic Mental Patient." In *The Chronic Mental Patient,* edited by J. A. Talbott. pp. 11-37. Washington, D.C.: The American Psychiatric Association.

Myers, J. K., and L. L. Bean. 1964 *A Decade Later: A Follow-Up of Social Class and Mental Illness.* New York: Wiley.

Rosenblatt, A., and J. E. Mayer. 1974. "The Recidivism of Mental Patients: A Review of Past Studies." *American Journal of Orthopsychiatry* 44, no. 5 (October): 697–706.

Sanders, R.; R. S. Smith; and B. S. Weinman. 1967. *Chronic Psychoses and Recovery.* San Francisco: Jossey-Bass.

Turner, J. C., and I. Shifren. 1979. "Community Support Systems: How Comprehensive?" In *New Directions for Mental Health Services,* edited by H. R. Lamb, vol 2, pp. 1–13. San Francisco: Jossey-Bass.

Turner, J. C., and W. J. TenHoor. 1978. "The NIMH Community Support Program: Pilot Approach to a Needed Social Reform." *Schizophrenia Bulletin* 4, no. 3: 319–48.

7 FACTORS AFFECTING ADJUSTMENT TO COMMUNITY LIVING

The emergence in the 1970s of a variety of community alternatives for the chronically mentally ill was accompanied by significant advances in scientific knowledge about the correlates of successful adjustment to community living (Bachrach 1976; Talbott 1979; Department of Health and Human Services 1980). Despite these recent advances, the literature about deinstitutionalization continues to lack a coherent theoretical perspective that can account for differences between persons with chronic mental disorders in their adjustment to community living. Under what conditions are persons with chronic mental disorders succeeding in finding remunerative employment or in working without pay at least part time? Under what conditions are such persons actively involved with a network of friends and relatives and participating in social and recreational activities? In an era in which hospitalization represents an alternative of last resort, what are the conditions that lead to episodic hospitalization or to crisis assistance in community-based settings?

In order to address these questions, the current chapter develops a theoretical model of community adjustment and tests the model with data descriptive of a representative sample of clients participating in the National Institute of Mental Health (NIMH) Community Support Program (CSP). According to the model, poor community adjustment results from deficits in basic living skills, behaviors and traits which offend others, and somatic problems which restrict independent activity. The model is used in the prediction of clients' work status, social activity, need for psychiatric hospitalization, and emergency client contacts. Rela-

Beth Sycamore assisted in the analysis of the data for this chapter.

tionships among these dependent variables are also examined. In addition, the explanatory model is applied to a subsample of clients with jobs in order to predict type of work, number of hours worked per week, and earned income.

Theoretical Development

In striving to predict different facets of community adjustment, we shall focus on individual client attributes which, at least to some degree, can be modified by programmatic intervention. One such attribute is basic living skills. The lack of appropriate skills for everyday living is a major barrier to effective community adjustment. As Mechanic has noted in relation to the problems psychotic patients experience in the community, the absence of appropriate skills makes it difficult for chronically mentally ill individuals "to find and maintain employment, to establish functional interpersonal relationships, to enjoy adequate living quarters, and to avoid difficulties with the authorities" (1978: 311).

What tends to be viewed as a mundane problem by persons possessing appropriate skills may be experienced as a crisis by persons who lack the crucial problem-solving skills. Whatever the source of the inadequacy, whether the appropriate skills were never present or whether they eroded as a function of institutionalization, the absence of appropriate living skills in patients in the community impedes satisfactory community adjustment. Because of its significance for community living, training in basic skills represents a major approach to the psychosocial treatment of the chronically mentally ill (Stein and Test 1976; Goldstein et al. 1976; Mosher and Keith 1980).

A second individual attribute hypothesized to exacerbate the problems patients face in the community concerns the normative quality of their behavior in so far as the behavior of the chronically mentally ill exceeds the community's tolerance limits. The normative quality of patient behavior suggests the patient's propensity to violate strongly held expectations and, in so doing, to shock, threaten, or otherwise disrupt the conventional flow of community life. The more inappropriately a patient behaves, the slimmer are his or her chances of finding and keeping a job, making friends and being accepted into informal social groups, and avoiding community reactions that could lead to hospitalization (Freeman and Simmons 1963; Eaton 1980; Mechanic 1980). Somatic problems that impair individual functioning may also exacerbate attempts to fulfill the demands of community living. While the evidence is far from complete, there are indications that, compared with the general population, persons with mental disorders have more chronic medical problems and shorter life expectancies (Babigian and Odoroff 1969; Eastwood 1975; Karasu et al. 1980). Though we would expect patients with chronic medical problems to make poorer adjustments to community living than patients who are physically healthy, this issue has (to the best of our knowledge) not been systematically examined.

In sum, it is hypothesized that successful community adjustment is threatened by impoverished skill repertoires related to the requirements of everyday living, by behavioral patterns or traits that are bizarre or in other ways violate strongly held social expectations, and by somatic problems that restrict or impair independent activity. No hypotheses are formulated about the relative importance of these three types of independent variables, though it is likely that their relative priority will vary depending on whether the indicator of community adjustment is work status, social activity, psychiatric hospitalization, or emergency client contact.

The theoretical model can be expressed as:

$$zca_i = B_a zls + B_b zbp + B_c zsp,$$

where zca_i are standardized scores representing the four different indicators of community adjustment (work status, social activity, psychiatric hospitalization, emergency client contact), zls are standardized scores representing basic living skills, zbp are standardized scores representing behavioral problems, and zsp are standardized scores representing somatic problems. In this standardized equation, B_a, B_b, and B_c are Beta coefficients denoting the direction and magnitude of each of the effects. Estimation of this model with actual data will enable us to assess the independent effects of basic living skills, behavioral problems, and somatic problems on the four indicators of community adjustment. Four different regression equations will be computed.

Another objective is to apply the theoretical model to a sub-sample of persons with chronic mental disorders who are currently working. In these analyses the key dependent variables will be type of job (in terms of level of independence), number of hours worked per week, and earned income. The results will suggest whether the same variables that predict work status also predict level of independence and productivity, and whether there are any predictors that are unique to the subsample of "working" persons. Finally, while the theoretical model is assumed to be additive, we shall explore possible interactions between the main independent variables in both the total sample and subsample analyses.

METHODS

The data come from a sample of 1,471 persons with chronic mental disorders, constituting 34.3 percent of the estimated 4,288 persons receiving NIMH-sponsored community support services in 1980. The data were collected using the Uniform Client Data Instrument (UCDI) developed by NIMH for use in the evaluation of the CSP. The UCDI allows for client descriptive data to be provided by case managers. A total of 248 case managers participated in the study. Each case manager provided a list of client numbers and, from among these numbers, a random sample of clients were selected for inclusion in the study. Because the sampling fraction was not constant across sites, fractional weights were applied to all data elements in order to ensure that the data were representative of the total population of CSP clients.[1]

The data collection sites included three "replication" sites in addition to the original fifteen funded local demonstrations. The participating sites were located in Redding, California; Santa Rosa, California; Denver, Colorado; Miami, Florida; Schenectady, New York; Syracuse, New York; Wingdale, New York; Brockton, Massachusetts; Ann Arbor, Michigan; St. Louis, Missouri; Minneapolis, Minnesota; Billings, Montana; Huron, South Dakota; Mitchell, South Dakota; Yankton, South Dakota; Dallas, Texas; Wichita Falls, Texas; and Washington, D.C. Two visits were made to each site in early 1980 in order to acquaint the case managers with the data collection plans and to familiarize local staff with the questionnaire. In the actual study, case managers were encouraged to consult existing records and other staff members as necessary in order to complete the UCDIs. Procedures were also established to ensure the anonymity of the client data. Data collection commenced in the spring of 1980, soon after the second field visit by a representative of the research team.

Independent Measures

This section provides an overview of the measurement of the three independent variables in the analytic model: basic living skills, behavioral problems, and somatic problems.

The Index of Basic Living Skills. The data for this index were drawn from thirteen items in the UCDI covering a variety of skills that are important for community living. The items were: maintains personal hygiene, dresses self, walks/gets around, maintains adequate diet, prepares/obtains own meals, maintains prescribed program of medication, performs household chores, goes shopping, uses available transportation on familiar routes, uses available transportation on unfamiliar routes, manages available funds, secures necessary support services, and is able to verbalize needs. Responses to these items were recoded into a four-point scale, with 0 equaling *acts independently,* 1 equaling *needs minor assistance or supervision,* 2 equaling *has difficulty and needs assistance,* and 3 equaling *is unable or unwilling to act independently.* In order to construct the index of basic living skills for each client, a count was made of the number of skill areas in which the client did not act independently, and this total was multiplied by an average (mean) severity score based on all thirteen items. The resulting index had a possible range of 0 to 39, with higher scores indicating more deficits in basic living skills.

The Index of Behavioral Problems. This index is based on fourteen items included in the UCDI. The items were: was incontinent, wandered/loitered, had trouble at work or school, caused complaints from household, caused community complaints, engaged in inappropriate sexual behavior, exhibited temper tantrums, had trouble with the law, destroyed/stole property, abused alcohol, abused drugs (includes legal, illegal, prescribed and nonprescribed drugs), made suicidal threats or attempts, engaged in bizarre behavior, and used matches, cigarettes, or fire hazardously.

Responses to these items were recoded into a four-point scale, with 0 equaling *no problem,* 1 equaling *minor problem,* 2 equaling *moderate problem,*and 3 equaling *serious problem.* In order to construct a summary index, the same procedure was followed as already described for the index of basic living skills. For every client, the total number of behavioral problem areas was computed, and the result was multipled by a mean severity score based on all fourteen items. The resulting scores represented the behavioral problem index, with higher scores indicating a higher prevalence of behaviors likely to be offensive to community residents. The index had a potential range of 0 to 42.

The Index of Somatic Problems.   This is a simple summated index based upon responses to a checklist of fifteen chronic medical problems likely to interfere with clients' daily activities or functioning. Using the UCDI to provide client-descriptive data, case managers checked whether or not the client had chronic medical problems in each of the following areas: impaired motor control, degenerative joint disease, circulatory and heart disorders, hypertension, respiratory disorders, cancer, diabetes, obesity/undernourished, medication side effects, skin disorder, convulsive disorder, developmental disability/mental retardation, blindness or severe visual impairment, deafness or severe hearing loss, and nonambulatory or major difficulty in ambulation. In addition, two other problem categories—digestive disorders, and dental/mouth—were derived from a content analysis of responses to a follow-up probe concerning other physiological disorders not included in the original list. Each client received a total score representing the actual number of chronic problems. The potential range of this index was from 0 to 17. Higher scores indicated poorer physical health.

Dependent Measures

Next, the measures of community adjustment are reviewed. These measures were used to describe variation between clients in work status, social activities, psychiatric hospitalization, and emergency client contacts. All data come from the UCDI, as provided by the case managers.

Work status. This is a three-point scale that combined two sources of information from the UCDI: whether the client had any job at all at the time of the study (including nonpaid work); and whether the client earned income. If the client was not working, a score of 0 was assigned. If the client was working, but earning no real income, a score of 1 was assigned. If the client was both working and earning income, a score of 2 was assigned. Approximately 26 percent of the total sample was currently working, at least part time, and 54.7 percent of the employed group was earning income.

The Index of Social Activity. This index is based on seven items reflecting how often the client took part in social activities in a recent typical week. The following items were included: socialized with family members; socialized with friends; engaged in any scheduled daytime activity; engaged in recreational activities at home, other than TV or radio; engaged *alone* in recreational activities outside the home, for example, movies, sports, lectures, visit parks; engaged *with others* in recreational activities outside the home, for example, movies, sports, lectures, visit parks; and attended clubs, lodge or other meetings. In order to construct this index, the total number of categories in which there was evidence of social activity was computed and this total score was multiplied by the mean frequency of social activity based on all seventeen items. The mean frequency of social activity was measured on a five-point scale, with 0 equaling *never,* 1 equaling *once a week or less,* 2 equaling 2 to 3 *days a week,* 3 equaling 4 to 5 *days a week,* and 4 equaling 6 to 7 *days a week.* The potential range of the social activity index was from 0 to 28, with higher scores indicating more social activity.

Psychiatric Hospitalization. The measure of hospitalization was based on the question: "In the last twelve months, how many weeks did the client receive hospitalization for a psychiatric condition?" In the analysis, the hospitalization data were collapsed into two categories with 0 equaling *no record of hospitalization in the last twelve months,* and 1 equaling *one or more admissions.*

Emergency Contacts.   In order to detect instances in which crises in social functioning were handled in community rather than hospital settings, an attempt was made to predict emergency client contacts. This item was drawn from the utilization section of the UCDI, and was subsumed under the more general category "Twenty-four Hour Quick Response Crisis Assistance." This item was measured dichotomously, with 0 equaling *no emergency contact* and 1 equaling *one or more emergency client contacts in the past month.*

RESULTS

Table 7–1 shows the descriptive statistics for the sample of 1,471 clients, weighted to reflect their representation in the total population of CSP clients. Examination of each of the independent variables in Table 7–1 reveals a skewed distribution of scores with substantial dispersion around the means.

Table 7–1 also shows the distribution of scores on the four measures of community adjustment. Approximately 74 percent of the clients were not working at all at the time of the study, and only 14.6 percent were earning income. The distribution of scores on the social activity index was also skewed toward the lower range. As expected, these individuals exhibited a relatively low level of social activity ($\overline{X}$ = 6.7 on a 28-point scale), though here too there was considerable variability around the mean (S.D. = 4.35). Table 7–1 also shows that about 31 percent of the clients had been hospitalized in the last twelve months, and that about 15 percent had received at least one emergency contact in the past month.

Table 7–2 shows the regression of each of the indicators of community adjustment on basic living skills, behavioral problems, and somatic problems. Because there were four indicators of community adjustment, there are four separate regression equations. The first equation examines clients' current work status as a function of the three predictors in the model. As Table 7–2 shows, all three variables were related in the expected direction to work status, and each of the standardized regression coefficients was statistically significant. The presence of appropriate basic living skills increased the probability that the client was presently

TABLE 7–1.   Descriptive Statistics for the Total Sample (N = 1,471).

Independent Variable	Coding Algorithm[a]	Mean	Standard Deviation
Living Skills	higher scores = more serious problems (0–39)	5.20	7.46
Behavioral Problems	higher scores = more serious problems (0–42)	1.25	3.07
Somatic Problems	higher scores = more chronic medical problems (0–17)	.78	1.27
Work status	0 = no work 1 = work/no earned income 2 = work/earned income	.39	.72
Social Activity	higher scores = more social activity (0–28)	6.71	4.35
Hospitalization	0 = no 1 = yes	.31	.43
Emergency Contact	0 = no 1 = yes	.15	.35

[a]Numbers in parentheses indicate possible range on index.

TABLE 7–2.   Community Adjustments as a Function of Living Skills, Behavioral Problems, and Somatic Problems (N = 1,471).

Independent Variable	Work status	Social Activity	Hospitalization	Emergency Contact
Living Skills	−.16[a]	−.22[a]	.05	.02
Behavioral Problems	−.08[a]	.04	.23[a]	.17[a]
Somatic Problems	−.09[a]	.04	−.06[a]	.005
R^2	.049	.047	.064	.030

Note: Each of the coefficients of determination (R^2) is significantly different from 0.
[a]$p < .05$

working and earning income. Similarly, low scores on the index of behavioral problems and low scores on the index of somatic problems also increased the probability of remunerative employment. Of the three predictors, the index of basic living skills was the strongest predictor of work status. While each of the independent variables exercised statistically significant effects, the amount of variance explained by the total model is low (R^2 = .049).

The second equation in Table 7–2 shows the results when the social activity index was regressed against the same three independent variables. Only basic living skills was significantly related to social activity. As for the direction of the relationship, the results show that the presence of skills appropriate for daily living was associated with higher levels of social and leisure-time activity. This is consistent with the prediction, which was based on the assumption that appropriate skills increase the probability of satisfactory community adjustment. This equation accounted for about 5 percent of the variance in social activity.

A different pattern is evident from the third and fourth equations. When psychiatric hospitalization in the last twelve months is regressed against the model's three predictors, the predominant predictor is the index of behavioral problems (see equation 3). Similarly, a positive relationship is detected between behavioral problems and the occurrence of emergency client contacts (see equation 4). As expected, the probability of both hospitalization and emergency contacts was increased to the extent that the client behaved in ways that exceeded the limits of community tolerance. Analysis of individual items comprising the fourteen-item index of behavioral problems showed the strongest associations between hospitalization and the following behaviors: "wandered/loitered" (r = .20), "exhibited temper tantrums" (r = .24), "caused complaints from household" (r = .21), and "engaged in bizarre behaviors" (r = .23). Emergency client contacts was most strongly correlated with "caused complaints from household" (r = .23) and "engaged in bizarre behavior" (r = .24), in addition to "made suicide threats or attempts" (r = .20).

By contrast with equations 1 and 2, in which basic living skills was the best predictor of work status and social activity, scores on the living skills index were random with respect to the probability of hospitalization and emergency client contacts during the period under study. The regression of psychiatric hospitalization on client attributes did detect a statistically significant, though modest, effect of somatic problems on hospitalization (Beta = −.06). This result ran counter to the hypothesis, however, showing that more (rather than fewer) somatic problems tended to reduce the probability of psychiatric hospitalization in the prior year. The direction of this relationship was unexpected, and the finding is not readily interpretable. Although equation 3 accounted for only 6.4 percent of the variance in hospitalization, and equation 4 explained only 3 percent of the variance in emergency client contacts, both r^2 statistics are significantly different from 0.

Relations among Indicators of Community Adjustment

Are persons who are well adjusted in terms of one dimension of community life also likely to be well adjusted in respect to other dimensions? One would expect to find some consistency across dimensions simply by virtue of the relationships of clients' living skills, behavioral problems, and somatic problems with the different facets of community adjustment. But is there some interdependency between the different facets of community adjustment that is independent of variation in client attributes? In order to examine this issue, a series of partial correlations was computed, controlling for clients' status on the indices of basic living skills, behavioral problems, and somatic problems. The results are presented in Table 7–3.

TABLE 7–3. Partial Correlations between Four Indicators of Community Adjustment[a] (N = 1,471).

	Gainful Employment	Social Activity	Hospitalization in Past Year
Social Activity	.11[b]		
Hospitalization in Past Year	−.06[c]	.01	
Emergency Assistance in Past Month	.03	.07[c]	.10[b]

[a]The control variables were basic living skills, behavioral problems, and somatic problems.
[b]p < .001
[c]p < .01

Inspection of the matrix of partial correlation coefficients in Table 7–3 shows that four of the six coefficients are statistically significant, though none of the associations are particularly strong. As expected, engaging in social activities is associated with remunerative employment (p < .001), and employment is also associated with decreased probability of a psychiatric hospitalization during the prior twelve months (p < .01). A recent hospitalization, as expected, tends to enhance the probability of one or more emergency client contacts within the past month (p < .001). But, unexpectedly, higher levels of social activity were associated with *increased* likelihood of emergency contacts.

One interpretation of the latter finding is that higher levels of social activity may involve more obvious behavioral manifestations of mental disorder. A related interpretation is that stress accompanying social situations may precipitate pathological behavior which, in turn, enhances the need for emergency assistance. It should be emphasized, however, that the sample is extremely heterogeneous, and that many persons experienced high levels of social activity without requiring emergency assistance.

There was no significant relationship between emergency client contacts in the past month and remunerative employment, or between recent psychiatric hospitalization and current level of social activity. These results lend further support to the view of community adjustment as a complex and multifaceted variable involving relatively distinct yet interdependent dimensions (Minkoff 1978).

Predictors of Type of Job, Number of Hours, and Earned Income

A final objective of the present research was to apply the theoretical model to the subsample of "working" persons in order to refine our understanding of work performance in this client population. These analyses focus on a subsample of 371 persons (approximately 26% of the total sample) who were reported to be currently working. Three indicators of work performance are analyzed: type of job, number of hours per week, and monthly earned income.

The coding algorithms and descriptive statistics for these variables are shown in Table 7–4. Type of job was coded in terms of level of independence, with 1 equaling *sheltered workshop,* 2 equaling *transitional employment, prevocational training, and volunteer positions,* and 3 equaling *competitive job obtained on the open market.*[2] The average number of hours worked per week was coded on a three-point scale, with 1 equaling *under 20 hours* (*part time*), 2 equaling 20 to 34 *hours* (*part time*), and 3 equaling 35 *and over* (*full time*). Earned monthly income was coded as a dichotomous variable, with 0 equaling *none* and 1 equaling *some earned income.* Table 7–4 also includes the coding algorithm and the descriptive statistics for the index of social activities. This variable was included because prior analyses showed that it was related to work status in the total sample (see Table 7–3).

It is instructive to compare the means in Table 7–4 for living skills, behavioral problems, and somatic problems with the corre-

TABLE 7–4.   Descriptive Statistics for the Subsample of "Working" Persons (N = 371).

Independent Variable	Coding Algorithm[a]	Mean	Standard Deviation
Living Skills	higher scores = more serious problems (0–39)	3.05	4.96
Behavioral Problems	higher scores = more serious problems (0–42)	.71	1.97
Somatic Problems	higher scores = more chronic medical problems (0–17)	.62	1.08
Type of Job	1 = sheltered workshop 2 = transitional, training & volunteer 3 = competitive	2.05	.88
Number of Hours	1 = under 20 hrs. (part time) 2 = 20–34 hrs. (part time) 3 = 35 and over (full time)	1.95	.81
Earned Income	0 = no 1 = yes	.15	.35
Social Activity	higher scores = more social activity (0–28)	7.84	4.00

[a]Numbers in parentheses indicate possible range on index.

sponding means in Table 7–1. Since Table 7–1 is based on the total sample, whereas Table 7–4 is based only on persons who were working at the time of the study, we would expect the latter to show fewer problems in basic living skills, fewer behavioral problems, fewer somatic problems, and more social activity. Comparison of the means shows that this is in fact what occurred. Additional analyses comparing working versus nonworking clients reveal statistically significant differences in respect to all four variables noted above. Working clients had fewer deficits in basic living skills ($\overline{X}$= 3.05, S.D. = 4.96 versus $\overline{X}$= 5.92, S.D. = 8.00, p < .001), fewer behavioral problems ($\overline{X}$= .71, S.D. = 1.97 versus $\overline{X}$= 1.44, S.D. = 3.34 p < .001), fewer somatic problems ($\overline{X}$= .62, S.D. = 1.08, versus $\overline{X}$= .83, S.D. = 1.33, p < .01), and a *higher* level of social activity ($\overline{X}$= 7.84, S.D. = 4.00 versus $\overline{X}$= 6.33, S.D. = 4.40, p < .001).

Table 7–5 presents the regression of type of job on living skills, behavioral problems, somatic problems, and social activities (see model 1). The results show that both living skills and somatic problems are strongly related to type of job. The greater the problems related to everyday living skills, and the more somatic problems, the less likely it is to find clients engaging in independent work activity. Neither the index of behavioral problems nor the index of social activities contributed significantly to the prediction of type of job. This regression equation accounted for al-

TABLE 7–5.   Predictors of Type of Job, Number of Hours, and Earned Income among "Working" Persons (N = 371).

| | Beta Coefficients Indicator of Productivity | | |
Independent Variable	Type of Job	Number of Hours	Earned Income
Living Skills	−.35[a]	−.17[a]	−.23[a]
Behavioral Problems	−.06	.12[a]	−.04
Somatic Problems	−.27[a]	−.20[a]	−.30[a]
Social Activities	.03	−.003	.002
R^2	.238	.082	.168

Note: Each of the coefficients of determination is significantly different from 0.
[a] p < .05

most 24 percent of the variance in type of job, far more than any of the models presented in Table 7–2.

The second model in Table 7–5 shows the regression of number of hours of work per week on living skills, behavioral problems, somatic problems, and social activities. This equation explained 8.2 percent of the variance in the dependent variable. The results reveal significant effects for living skills and somatic problems, each in the expected direction, but no relationship between social activities and hours worked. It is noteworthy that, compared to model 1, the relative priority of living skills and somatic problems is altered, with somatic problems emerging as the best predictor. The results further show an unexpected relationship between high scores on the behavioral problem index and more hours worked per week.

If behavioral problems are viewed as a possible outcome of long and stressful work days, one possibility is that longer work days evoked more disruptive behavior. In order to explore this possibility, the index of behavioral problems was regressed on number of hours worked, in addition to the other two indicators of productivity. Consistent with the interpretation suggested above, the results show that working longer hours does increase the probability of higher than average scores on the index of behavioral problems (Beta = .15, $p < .01$). The results also indicated that behavioral problems were most common in the least independent work settings (Beta = $-.16$, $p < .01$).

The final model in Table 7–5 shows the regression of earned monthly income on the four independent variables. It is important to note that this dependent measure is not redundant with the two prior measures of productivity. About one in four persons working in sheltered workshops (the least independent work setting) were paid for their labor, and there was also considerable variation in earned monthly income as a function of number of hours worked; 20.5 percent of the clients who were working full time (at least thirty-five hours a week) did not earn income, and 39.4 percent who were working under twenty hours per week were paid.

In the prediction of earned monthly income, somatic problems once again emerged as the strongest predictor, followed by the index of basic living skills. Among individuals who worked at the time of the study, the better their living skills, and the better their physical health, the higher was the probability that they earned monthly income. Neither behavioral problems nor social activities contributed to the prediction of earned monthly income. This final model explained 16.8 percent of the variance.

Tests for Interactions

Though the model was conceptualized to be additive, we nevertheless tested for interactions between living skills, behavioral problems, and somatic problems. We conducted these interaction tests in respect to the four dependent variables considered in the total sample (N = 1,471) and the three dependent variables examined in the subsample (N = 371).

Using multiplicative terms to denote all possible two- and three-way interactions among the three independent variables, we examined a total of twenty-eight interaction terms. The main effects for the three independent variables were also included in each equation. Examination of the results showed no dramatic increases in the proportion of variance explained when the multiplicative interaction terms were included in the regression equations. The three main effects continued to account for most of the variance. Only six out of the twenty-eight interaction terms examined were statistically significant, and those that were significant failed to show a consistent pattern.

SUMMARY AND DISCUSSION

This paper has drawn on data provided by case managers about a representative sample of individuals participating in the NIMH CSP. The major purpose of the analysis was to test a linear model of community adjustment which highlights the potential significance of individual client attributes. According to this model, the extent of community adjustment is hypothesized to be affected by basic living skills, behavioral problems, and somatic problems. The lack of appropriate skills for daily living, the presence of specific behaviors which upset community residents, and physical health problems that restrict independent activity are all conceived as impediments to satisfactory community adjustment.

The theoretical model was applied to four facets of community adjustment. The first two of these, work status and social activity, describe the fabric of clients' lives and the quality of their functioning in the community. Two other indicators, psychiatric hospitalization and emergency client contacts, point to instances of social breakdown and personal crisis. At issue was the extent to which work status, social activity, psychiatric hospitalization, and emergency client contact could be predicted by knowledge of clients' basic living skills, behavioral problems, and somatic problems, and what the relative importance of each of these predictors would be.

Although the amount of variance explained was not large, and the predictive value of the model is thereby limited, the results do show some statistically significant findings. Work status is significantly affected by all three predictors, as expected, but the best predictor is basic living skills. Those clients who were rated by their case managers as in need of assistance in order to fulfill a variety of everyday living needs were least likely to be gainfully employed. Basic living skills was also the main predictor of social activity. As hypothesized, those individuals who were most able to take care of themselves in terms of basic everyday needs were also the more socially active. Neither behavioral nor somatic problems was predictive of social activity in this client population. Whereas the index of basic living skills was the best predictor of work status and social activity, the same index was not significantly related either to hospitalization or to emergency client contact. The best predictor, by far, of the latter dependent variables was the number and severity of behavioral problems.

We were also interested in relationships between the four indicators of community adjustment, controlling for the measured variation in living skills, behavioral problems, and somatic problems. While four of the six partial correlations were statistically significant, none of the correlations were strong, and in general the results supported a view of community adjustment as involving relatively distinct yet interdependent dimensions. The strongest associations were between remunerative employment and a higher than average level of social activity, and between psychiatric hospitalization in the prior year and one or more emergency client contacts within the last month.

In addition to the analysis of community adjustment in the total sample, the model was also used to explain work performance in a subsample of clients who had jobs at the time of the study. The aspects of work performance studied were type of work (in terms of level of independence), number of hours per week, and earned income.

The most striking result in these analyses was the emergence of somatic problems as a significant predictor of work-related performance. The index of somatic problems was significantly related to all three dependent measures, and it was the strongest predictor of number of hours and earned income. For the working client, the presence of somatic problems clearly impedes performance on the job. The sicker the individual, the less likely he or she was to secure a job in the competitive market, to work full time, and to earn income. In addition to the effect of somatic problems, work performance was also affected by living skills, and the effect of living skills on type of job was especially strong.

Implications

Those who work in CSSs, program administrators, case managers, and specialists in direct client services, as well as evaluators, are concerned with enhancing the adjustment of chronic clients to life in the community. For most practitioners, this general objective translates into helping clients to secure remunerative employment, enrich their social lives and their use of leisure time, and avoid personal crises that might otherwise lead to emergency interventions and hospitalization. Yet, from an evaluation standpoint, little is presently known about how best to assess client needs and develop optimal approaches in individual cases (Schulberg 1979).

From the results of the current study, one could infer a hierarchy of deficits and needs, with basic living skills at the base, followed by behavioral problems and somatic problems. Clinical focuses might vary accordingly, depending on that facet of community adjustment which is of concern. If the goal is to enrich the client's connection to the community through work and social activity, then it is basic living skills that need to be brought into focus. If, on the other hand, the goal is to reduce the client's need for emergency services and to prevent psychiatric hospitalization, then the results of the present study suggest that it is behavioral problems that need to be brought into focus. For clients who are already working, and for whom improved work performance is sought, attention must be given to somatic problems in addition to basic living skills, In this manner, the results of the current study are suggestive of those areas where attention and additional effort are best focused in order to achieve positive changes in clients' adjustment to community living.

Implicit in this analysis is the assumption that basic living skills, behavioral problems, and somatic problems are all "manipulatable" variables, which may be affected by clinical and programmatic interventions. Unfortunately, the cross-sectional character of the current study makes it impossible to assess change over time in living skills, behavioral problems, and somatic problems. Longitudinal data are required to provide a more direct test of the hypothesis that the provision of community support services will lead to *changes* in these three client attributes which, in turn, will result in the expected improvements in community adjustment.

Another caveat surrounding the practical implications of the research findings is that, in general, the theoretical model did not account for substantial variance in community adjustment. With the exception of the regression of type of job in which we succeeded in accounting for almost 24 per cent of the variance, and the regression of earned income, which showed an R^2 of about 17 per cent, the R^2 statistics were all under .10. The low R^2 statistics are probably due to a variety of factors including heterogeneity in this client population, skewed distributions of key variables, and unreliability of measurement. Evidence of this latter source of error was detected in reanalyses of the specific models based only on questionnaires in which the case manager reported knowing the client "very well." As expected, these equations explained somewhat more of the variance in the various indicators of community adjustment (results not shown).

Yet another caveat concerns the generalizability of the results. While these data may very well constitute the best national data currently available about the chronically mentally ill in community settings, it is nevertheless inappropriate to generalize the results beyond the finite population of CSP clients. To generalize beyond this finite population is to encounter all the hazards in making inferences based on "treated cases." As is now well known, such cases may differ in a variety of ways from the larger population (Mechanic 1980). Considering that little is currently known about the similarities and differences between CSP clients and other chronically mentally ill persons, considerable caution should be exercised in any effort to extrapolate the present results to other clinical settings and client populations.

Whatever the ambiguities in the present study, it is reasonably clear from the results that community adjustment is not a single variable, and that distinct client attributes are related to different facets of adjustment. In this way, the results are similar to related research on client satisfaction which has also been shown to have distinct dimensions with different causal antecedents (Polansky and Kounin 1956; Tessler 1975).

The current investigation has focused on client attributes which impede satisfactory community adjustment. In so doing, we have held structural factors constant. Structural barriers to community adjustment, such as lack of community acceptance of the chronic patient, unavailability of appropriate housing, the poor quality of psychosocial rehabilitation programs, and limited access to third-party reimbursement for needed services are extremely important, and need to be examined in conjunction with client attributes in future studies of factors affecting clients' adjustment to community living.

NOTES

1. In order to compute appropriate weights for the 1,471 cases, separate weights were computed for each local demonstration site and then multipled by each of the data elements used in this analysis. The computation of the weights involved the following three discrete steps:

    (1) $\dfrac{N_i}{N}$

    (2) $\dfrac{N_i}{N} \times 1471 = N_e$

    (3) Weight $= \dfrac{N_e}{N_a}$

    Where: N_i = number of clients served at the local demonstration site; N = number of clients in the total population (4,288); N_e =

number of expected clients to be sampled at the local demonstration site; and N_a = number of actual clients sampled at the local demonstration site. According to the formula, each weight was a function of the expected number of clients divided by the number for whom data were actually secured. Each weight was rounded to the fourth decimal.

2. Partial lists of the actual job descriptions for each of the foregoing categories of work are available in Appendix E of the Final Report by Market Facts, Inc., entitled *Collaborative Data Collection and Analysis for Community Support Program Demonstration Projects* (Bernstein, Love, and Davis 1981).

REFERENCES

Babigian, H. M., and C. L. Odoroff. 1969. "The Mortality Experience of a Population with Psychiatric Illness." *American Journal of Psychiatry* 126, No. 4 (October): 470–80.

Bachrach, Leona L. 1976. *Deinstitutionalization: An Analytic Review and Sociological Perspective.* DHEW Publication No. (ADM) 76–351. Washington, D.C.: Government Printing Office.

Bernstein, Alice G.; Robert Love; and Glenn E. Davis, 1981. *Collaborative Data Collection and Analysis for Community Support Program Demonstration Projects.* NIMH Report No. 79-0031 (OP). Rockville, Md.: Mental Health.

Department of Health and Human Services. 1980. *Toward a National Plan for the Chronically Mentally Ill.* DHHS Publication No. (ADM) 81–1007. Washington, D.C.: Government Printing Office.

Eastwood, M. R. 1975. *The Relation between Physical and Mental Illness.* Toronto: University of Toronto Press.

Eaton, William W. 1980. *The Sociology of Mental Disorders.* New York: Praeger.

Freeman, Howard E., and Ozzie G. Simmons. 1963. *The Mental Patient Comes Home.* New York: Wiley.

Goldstein, Arnold P.; Robert P. Sprafkin; and N. Jane Gershaw. 1976. *Skill Training for Community Living.* New York: Permagon.

Karasu, Toksoz B.; Stuart A. Waltzman; Jean-Pierre Lindenmayer; and Peter J. Buckley. 1980. "The Medical Care of Patients with Psychiatric Illnesses." *Hospital and Community Psychiatry* 31, No. 7 (July): 463–72.

Mechanic, David. 1978. "Alternatives to Mental Hospitalization: A Sociological Perspective." In *Alternatives to Mental Hospitalization,* edited by Leonard I. Stein and Mary Ann Test, pp. 309–20. New York: Plenum Press.

————. 1980. *Mental Health and Social Policy.* Second Edition. Englewood Cliffs, New Jersey: Prentice Hall.

Minkoff, Kenneth. 1978. "A Map of the Chronic Mental Patient." In *The Chronic Mental Patient: Problems, Solutions and Recommendations for a Public Policy,* edited by J. A. Talbott, pp. 11–37. Washington, D.C.: The American Pyschiatric Association.

Mosher, L. R., and S. J. Keith. 1980. "Psychosocial Treatment: Individual, Group, Family, and Community Support Approaches." *Schizophrenia Bulletin* 6, No. 1: 10–41.

Polansky, N., and J. Kounin. 1956. "Clients' Reactions to Initial Interviews: A Field Study." *Human Relations* 9, No. 3: 237–264.

Schulberg, H. G. 1979. "Community Support Programs: Program Evaluation and Public Policy." *American Journal of Psychiatry* 136, No. 11 (November): 1433–37.

Stein, Leonard I., and Mary Ann Test. 1976. "Training in Community Living: One-Year Evaluation." *The American Journal of Psychiatry 133, No. 8 (August):* 917–18.

Talbott, J. A., ed. 1978. *The Chronic Mental Patient: Problems, Solutions, and Recommendations for a Public Policy.* Washington, D.C.: American Psychiatric Association.

Tessler, Richard C. 1975. "Clients' Reactions to Initial Inteviews: Determinants of Relationship-Centered and Problem-Centered Satisfaction." *Journal of Counseling Psychology* 22, No. 3 (May): 187–91.

Turner, Judith, and William TenHoor. 1978. "The NIMH Community Support Program: Pilot Approach to a Needed Social Reform." *Schizophrenia Bulletin* 4, No. 3: 319–48.

IV ASSESSING COMMUNITY SUPPORT PROGRAMS

8 ASSESSING THE NEED FOR COMMUNITY SUPPORTS

John W. Ashbaugh

The importance of assessing the need of severely and chronically mentally ill persons for community support services was well stated by Judith Turner, director of the National Institute of Mental Health's (NIMH's) Community Support Program (CSP):

> In order to reconsider federal policy and its impact on the mentally disabled more systematic information is needed on the total numbers of mentally disabled adults, their clinical and demographic characteristics, their current locus of services, the types of services they are now receiving, their quality of life and level of adjustment, the extent to which they are "inappropriately placed" either in hospitals or in the community, and the nature and extent of unmet service needs. (Turner and TenHoor 1978: 338).

Information on the service needs of severely and chronically mentally ill persons is no less important to state and local planners and policymakers. It is the basis for rational decisionmaking. Given the vagaries of the political process of course, information on needs may or may not be enough to influence decisions and to precipitate the desired actions. As is often the case, the needs information may simply be used to justify decisions already made or actions already taken. Needs information alone is insufficient to induce system reforms of benefit to the severely and chronically mentally ill. However, in the hands of committed and effective

141

system reformers, it can well make the difference between the reformers' success and failure.

In 1979, the CSP leadership recognized that little information existed on the service needs of severely and chronically mentally ill persons targeted by CSP, and that most CSP sites were having some difficulty developing such information for their own use, let alone that of the federal policymakers. Accordingly, the CSP commissioned The Human Services Research Institute (HSRI) to pull together existing information on the needs of the target population for immediate use by federal planners and policymakers, and to select from the universe of needs-assesment methods those that could be applied most effectively by state and local community support system (CSS) planners. The project is entitled, "Evaluation of the Community Support Program (CSP); Analysis of Needs Assessment Methodologies." The project is ongoing. This chapter summarizes the results of HSRI's review of needs-assessment methods. The review should be instructive to CSP policymakers, planners, administrators, and others engaging in, or using the results of, formalized assessments of the needs of the severely and chronically mentally ill persons.

For our purposes, needs assessment is broadly defined to include formalized studies to estimate: (1) the number of chronically mentally ill persons, served and unserved, (2) the clinical and demographic characteristics of these persons, (3) the service needs of these persons, and (4) the extent to which community support services are available, accessible, and utilized to meet these needs.

This chapter includes brief descriptions of five basic needs-assessment methods. It indicates the type of information that each can yield, and the uses and limitations of that information. In the case of the community survey method, two techniques are introduced that promise to make the method more useful for the purposes of assessing the needs of the chronically mentally ill population: composite estimation and synthetic estimation. The chapter also discusses the advantages inherent in using needs-assessment methods in combination and identifies some of the most logical combinations. In closing, it stresses the importance of working toward clear needs-assessment objectives, employing methods appropriate to these objectives, and having a clear understanding of the practical and technical limitations of the methods employed.

Five fundamental needs-assessment methods that might be applied in assessing the needs of the chronically mentally ill persons are:

1. *Sociodemographic Analyses*—Estimating the relative size and geographic distribution of the chronically mentally ill population in state and substate areas using sociodemographic indicies correlated with the incidence and prevalence of mental illness.
2. *Community Surveys*—Estimating the size, characteristics and service utilization patterns of the chronically mentally ill population, through surveys of general populations.
3. *Client Surveys*—Identifying or inferring the size, characteristics and service needs of chronically mentally ill persons receiving services, based on reviews of client case records, surveys of case managers, or surveys of the clients themselves.
4. *Service Provider Inventories*—Identifying or inferring the availability and accessibility of community support services to the target population through a census or sample survey of current and prospective community support providers.
5. *Key-Informant Surveys*—Identifying needs of the chronically mentally ill population or subpopulations and problems of developing the community support services through surveys of knowledgeable individuals.

The foregoing categories are distinguished primarily in terms of differences in data sources and collection methods. The distinctions between methods are useful for analytic purposes but somewhat artificial in that many of the methods overlap in practice.

SOCIODEMOGRAPHIC ANALYSES

This method involves the use of sociodemographic variables as indicators or correlates of need for services to the mentally ill. The method is well described by Hagedorn (1977: 80–81). It is based on studies that have shown that certain sociodemographic variables are highly correlated with the incidence of mental illness and concomitant need for services. (Hollingshead and Redlich 1958). The principal categories of social data used as surrogates for mental health need are income and employment, housing arrangements, sociodemographic characteristics, and measures of social problems.

Social indicators can be analyzed singly or in combination (e.g. age by marital status). The analyses can be simple or complex, using such statistical procedures as standard scoring, multiple regression, and factor analysis. Methods of data presentation typically include mapping, transparencies, or graphic presentations.

The NIMH has developed a data system called the Mental Health Demographic Profile System (MHDPS). The complete system includes 130 standard census items from the 1970 U.S. census that are believed to predict the risk of mental illness among different populations, and thus the relative need for mental health services (Redick, Goldsmith, and Unger 1971). An updated version of the MHDPS, using standard tape files from the 1980 census, will be available in 1982. Mustian and See (1973) and others have devised abbreviated versions of the MHDPS using smaller numbers of sociodemographic variables.

A major limitation of the method is that it yields relative, rather than absolute, estimates of the size (implied need) of the mentally ill population. Thus, while the MHDPS may be used to rank areas in order to implied need, it is but a floating foundation for mental health planning.

In order to apply a parallel method to estimate the relative size of the chronically mentally ill population from area to area, it would have to be demonstrated that consistent associations between particular socioeconomic variables and the prevalence of "chronic" mental illness (as determined from community surveys) exist from area to area. While this has not been demonstrated, it seems plausible that those same socioeconomic variables associated with a higher prevalence of mental illness (in general) would also be associated with a higher prevalence of chronic mental illness.

If considered alone, sociodemographic correlates of chronic mental illness may be quite misleading for purposes of state-level and small-area needs assessment. For instance it has been shown that deinstitutionalized, chronically mentally ill persons tend to cluster in communities adjacent to institutions (Segal and Aviram 1978). Thus one must be cautious when interpreting sociodemographic correlates of mental illness.

COMMUNITY SURVEYS

This methodological category involves the use of surveys of the general population to estimate the size, characteristics, and service-utilization patterns of the chronically mentally ill population. Such surveys can in addition elicit data on the attitudes and perceptions of consumers of mental health services. Community surveys can also help explain why chronically mentally ill persons utilize particular services and how they might be induced to alter their use to more effective and economic treatment modes. Finally, community surveys might be used to discover the unserved segment of the mentally ill who are not using services for economic, logistic, personal, or other reasons.

Community surveys do have major drawbacks. One problem with community surveys is that the validity of information obtained from respondents is difficult to establish. Validity problems result from response bias—for example, "yea saying," "nay saying," fear of stigma (Ware 1977; Sigelman et al. 1981), inaccurate respondent recall, and inadequate verbal skills (Warheit, Bell, and Schwab 1977).

Another problem encountered in community surveys is that undercounts or overcounts occur because of the difficulty distinguishing chronically mentally ill persons from other respondents. As explained in Chapter 1, the chronically mentally ill can be distinguished in terms of the diagnosis, disability, and duration of their disorders. By definition, a chronically mentally ill person is functionally impaired (disability) for reason of mental illness (diagnosis) for an extended period of time (duration). Unfortunately, existing community surveys provide only limited data about diagnosis, disability, and duration of illness, making estimates of the size of this population tentative at best.

The validity of respondent self-assessments and disclosures of mental disorders in response to surveys is open to question. For a variety of reasons (Phillips and Clancy 1970), studies of the validity of self-reports of mental illness as part of community surveys have alternatively been found to lead to underestimates (Trussell, Elinson, and Levin 1956) and overestimates of psychiatric disorders relative to clinical evaluations (Weissman, Myers, and Harding 1978).

Indirect measures of mental problems, particularly severe and chronic problems, also have been shown to have little validity. The scales currently used in community surveys to determine the presence of mental problems tend to concentrate heavily on the mild and moderate end of the symptom spectrum. As Jerome Frank puts it, they identify "demoralization," rather than mental illness (Link and Dohrenwend 1980). Dohrenwend and Crandell (1970) found that the well-known Langner Scale under-represented serious psychopathology. Tousignan, Denis, and Lachapelle (1974) maintain that the Health Opinion Survey scale does not distinguish persons with a permanent disabling mental disorder (such as schizophrenia, psychosis, or neurosis) from those with transitory emotional problems brought on by stress or health conditions. Dohrenwend (1972) concluded that the Mid-town Manhattan and Stirling County scales are also deficient in this regard.

Futhermore, the disability information available from existing community surveys is largely confined to physical dysfunction (e.g., lack of mobility, incontinence, etc.) and the inability to work. Information on the degree to which a person is functionally and socially incapacitated (e.g. unable to manage finances, to cook, to read, to socialize, etc.) has been quite limited to date. However, exceptions can be found among limited-area epidemiologic studies of mental illness (Hughes, et al. 1960; Srole et al. 1972; Langner and Michael 1963; Schwab et al. 1979; Regier 1979).

Community surveys generally yield little information on the duration of the respondent's mental illness and related disability. In most instances, the time window is twelve months or less.

A final problem is that the cost of conducting community surveys is enormous. The projected cost of conducting a 1982 postcensus survey of disabled persons was projected to be between ten and fifteen million dollars exclusive of design and pretest. Even then, in order to obtain a sufficient number of ill or disabled respondents to draw reasonably accurate inferences about their characteristics, service-utilization patterns, and attitudes, most health and disability surveys find it necessary to oversample. The oversample of ill or disabled individuals is drawn from such large data files as the census or the Health Interview Survey. And still, the sample data can be too thin to support reliable estimates of the size, characteristics, and service patterns of less-prevalent subpopulations such as the chronically mentally ill. Two relatively new techniques can and are being used to increase the reliability and utility of community survey data: composite estimation and synthetic estimation.

Composite Estimation

The composite estimation technique involves combining the estimates from two or more surveys, thus effectively enlarging the sample. The component estimates, of course, must be weighted. Estimates based on the survey thought to be more reliable are weighted more heavily; those based on the survey thought to be less reliable are weighted less heavily.

A variety of statistical schemes for weighting survey estimates using quantitative indices of the reliability of the component estimators have been explored (Efron and Morris 1973, 1975). A fairly common weighting procedure is to estimate the variance or mean squared error of the respective surveys by comparing the mean value of a common general population variable (e.g. age, marital status, education) to its "known value" as derived from the U.S. census or other established source. The survey estimates are then weighted inversely according to the mean squared errors of their respective estimates, that is, according to their relative reliability.

If the particular weighting scheme employed is valid, the composite estimates should be superior to the individual estimates. Generally speaking, survey results used in combination will increase the reliability of the estimate and reduce the survey sampling bias. The HSRI is currently in the process of combining selected characteristics of the chronically mentally ill population as estimated from the 1972 and 1978 Disability Surveys sponsored by the Social Security Administration (HSRI 1981).

Synthetic Estimation

The synthetic-estimation technique involves the use of sociodemographic-prevalence correlates and regression analyses to estimate the size and characteristics of the target population in one area based on the results of a community survey of the target population in another area (horizontal estimation) or in a larger, parent area (vertical estimation). Synthetic estimation is based on the assumption that the characteristic being estimated is correlated with selected demographic characteristics of the general population.

The inherent weakness of the synthetic estimators is that they all have an unknown and generally unestimable bias (Brock, French, and Peyton 1980). This weakness notwithstanding, synthetic estimation is a very economic and practical alternative to the conduct of multiple surveys in small areas, the cost of which can be even more prohibitive than those done nationally. Proportionate to the size of the state and local-area populations, larger samples are necessary in order to tap enough ill or disabled persons to draw reasonably accurate inferences about them.

A succinct explanation of the vertical type of synthetic estimation is provided by Schaible, Brock, and Schnack (1977). The first step in constructing a synthetic estimate is to create a cross-classification of demographic cells in such a way that the local-area population in each cell is known. The synthetic estimate for a local area is then formed by weighting a larger area estimate of the health characteristic for each demographic cell by the proportion of the local-area population in that cell and then summing over all cells.

This technique was first introduced in 1968 in a National Center for Health Statistics publication entitled, "Synthetic State Estimates of Disability." The report describes how the Health Interview Survey data are used to draw state estimates of disability. Since this time, reports have appeared describing the use of synthetic estimators for estimating state and local health characteristics (National Center for Health Statistics, 1977), unemployment and housing (Gonzalez and Hoza 1978; Schaible, Brock, and Schnack 1977), and income (Fay and Herriot 1979). Only recently, Holzer (1981) described how the horizontal method might be applied for estimating mental health characteristics in one local area based on community survey results in another area.

Currently, Holzer is estimating synthetically the size of the chronically mentally ill population residing in households in each state using prevalence rates derived from 1972 and 1978 Social

Security Administration (SSA) surveys of disabled and nondisabled persons (SSA 1975, 1979, and 1981). His work is part of a larger study by the HSRI (1981). The synthetic estimates are then to be adjusted to reflect differences between states in the proportion of chronically mentally ill persons who are institutionalized, and to distribute these estimates among substate levels adjusting for such factors as the tendency of chronically mentally ill persons to cluster around public mental hospitals and in transient, boarding-home areas. The study will also check the concurrent validity of these estimates, comparing them to available substate area estimates based directly on community or client surveys.

CLIENT SURVEYS

Surveys of clients generate descriptive information about the characteristics of the target population, the current service-utilization patterns, and the need for additional services based on a sample survey of types of individuals currently receiving services. These surveys can be used to collect a variety of types of information including clients' demographic and clinical characteristics, lifestyles and quality of life, utilization of services, unmet service needs, and satisfaction with existing services. Three data collection approaches may be used. They are: (1) client surveys, typically client interviews; (2) surveys of knowledgeable respondents (e.g., case managers or significant others) who report on individual clients; and (3) reviews of client records.

On the positive side, certain types of descriptive information about the target population can *only* be collected through the use of the client-survey method (e.g., the client's level of satisfaction with services received or quality of life measures). Moreover, client surveys permit a more extensive analysis of the relationships between client characteristics and service-utilization and service-demand patterns than do other assessment methods.

On the negative side, client surveys by definition ignore the unserved segment of the CSP population. Thus, the results cannot be used, in and of themselves, to make inferences about the overall chronically mentally ill population. The method may also be costly to apply depending on the mode of data collection employed and the size and geographic dispersion of the client sample. In addition, access to the client records is usually restricted for reasons of confidentiality. Finally, upon inspection, the client records and reports of the case managers and clients concerning the services provided and/or received are often found to be incomplete and inconsistent.

One variation of this method deserves mention: surveys of chronically mentally ill clients residing in mental hospitals and in other institutional care facilities intended to identify persons who are mentally and physically capable of returning to the community and to predict their demand for community support services. Such surveys pose the unique and difficult requirement of projecting the numbers of institutionalized persons who might return to the community if appropriate community supports can be found. Attempts to find client-situational characteristics (that can be captured via survey) to serve as predictors of client adaptation in the community have met with limited success (Ashbaugh, Hoff, and Bradley 1979; also see Chapter 7).

A predictor of community tenure having good face validity is the client's level of functioning—the client's ability to perform those activities of daily living necessary to survive in the community. In fact, this indicator is the keystone upon which many such methodologies are founded. Paradoxically, it is difficult to derive level-of-functioning measures that are good predictors of community adaptation since the way a client functions is largely dictated by his or her environment. The functioning alternatives open to a client in the institution are different and generally more restrictive than in the community. While the client's ability to cook his or her own meals may be a legitimate level-of-functioning indicator in a community living arrangement, it cannot be tested in an institution where meals are provided to the client. We are left then with only a few skills that apply in both environments—perhaps too few to predict client's success in the broad range of daily-living demands encountered in the community.

A more promising predictor of rehospitalization, or conversely, of successful adaption to community life, may be the degree to which the client exhibits problem behaviors. As explained in Chapter 7, the UCDI study suggests that problem behaviors (e.g.

self abuse, pyromania, exhibitionism) are indeed a better predictor of hospitalization than are the more commonly used level of functioning indices. Rightly or wrongly, more persons may be admitted to hospitals in order to control their problem behaviors than are admitted because they are unable to function in a community setting.

PROVIDER INVENTORIES

Service-provider inventories include surveys of agencies or individuals that are currently serving chronically mentally ill clients, or that might offer services to such individuals in the future. These methods are used to estimate the availability of services appropriate to serving the target population, to depict the current utilization patterns by members of the target population, and to indicate the unmet demand for additional services. The providers may also be asked to explain current service-utilization patterns and to identify barriers to the development and delivery of services to the target population. In this respect, the service providers are serving as key informants.

There are a number of problems associated with this methodological approach: The results pertaining to service availability are timebound, and the actual availability of services has often changed by the time the results are ready for use. Even when the data are timely, the level and type of available services are difficult to catalogue and aggregate because providers sometimes define their services quite differently. Providers might also overreport the level of services provided, and it is difficult, in the absence of agreed-upon norms, to gauge the effective capacity of nonresidential service providers. For instance, how many clients can be accommodated in a particular day-treatment program? How many clients can a case manager serve effectively? Yet another difficulty is that many of the providers targeted in these surveys, including Community Mental Health Centers, offer services to a wide range of clients, and their records may not isolate the services utilized by the chronically mentally ill, as distinct from other client groups.

SURVEYS OF KEY INFORMANTS

The key-informant method identifies the service problems and needs of the chronically mentally ill through surveys of knowledgeable individuals. The respondents are selected to represent a heterogeneity of experience and perspectives, and to bring some knowledge of the CSP population and its service needs. The key informants may be surveyed by mail, phone, or personal interviews and questioned about a wide range of issues pertaining to CSS service needs, delivery-system barriers and accessibility to services. The key-informant method is primarily a qualitative needs-assessment method, and the only method that serves to identify needs and problems directly. The method is discussed here as a separately administered procedure; however, as noted earlier, several groups of key informants may in fact be polled as part of the forementioned surveys. Case managers, therapists, and significant others may be surveyed as part of the client-targeted surveys, and service-provider staff may be surveyed as part of the provider inventories.

Employed at the outset of a needs-assessment effort, the key-informant technique can help identify the most significant needs and problems that might be confirmed subsequently using other quantititative needs-assessment techniques. In other words, the key informants can lead the larger needs-assessment effort into more productive channels. For example, a key informant might volunteer that there are too few qualified physicians in a given area of the state willing to treat chronically mentally ill clients on an outpatient basis. Steps may be then taken to obtain quantitative assessments of this problem.

The key-informant method can also be used at the end of a needs-assessment effort to help identify and explain the needs and problems embodied in the quantitative data obtained through other needs-assessment methods. For instance, a key informant asked to interpret the relatively high admission rates at a particular state mental hospital might offer the explanation that the private general hospitals in that area are not equipped to accept psychiatric inpatients requiring 24-hour supervision.

Another strength of this method is its economy. Unlike client surveys, community surveys, and other statistically based needs-assessment methods, key-informant surveys are more qualitative and exploratory in nature. The key-informant survey is relatively straightforward in design and yields results which can be interpreted directly. Accordingly, design and analysis costs are relatively low.

An important political advantage is that the key-informant survey can serve to make the key informants more cognizant of the special needs and problems of the chronically mentally disabled. In this manner, a key-informant survey can serve as a consensus-building tool among key actors in the system of care for the chronically mentally ill.

The inherent disadvantage of the method is that the results are often subjective and inconclusive. The key-informant sample is not intended to support statistically valid and reliable estimates of the magnitude of a service need or problem. The results of the key-informant survey are often anecdotal in nature and based on the subjective experience of the respondents; as such, the results cannot be meaningfully aggregated. Furthermore, as Warheit, Buhl, and Bell found in their Louisville survey, the key informants almost universally reported high levels of need in all problem/service areas. "This (low) level of discrimination . . . raises questions about the utility of their judgments for . . . planning purposes since it would be impossible to establish service priorities when the needs are so positively and uniformly reported" (1977: 12).

A related problem lies with the particular perspectives of key informants which reflect their personal and professional experiences and interests. In many cases, these perspectives reflect strong biases or rigid "tunnel visions." As a result it is often difficult to reconcile divergent positions among key informants and to establish points of consensus.

METHODOLOGICAL HYBRIDS

Clearly, any single method can provide only one part of the total needs-assessment picture. In order to obtain a more complete picture of the needs of the chronically mentally ill population, the needs-assessment methods are best employed in combination.

As indicated earlier, key-informant surveys are a natural complement to the other needs-assessment methods. Qualitative judgments of key informants can be used effectively to identify and to help explain the quantitative findings produced by the other needs-assessment methods (for example, client characteristics, service utilization patterns, service availability figures, etc.).

Provider inventories addressing the availability and accessibility of services are a logical complement to the client surveys, community surveys and sociodemographic analyses, all of which attempt to reflect on the demand, actual and potential (need), for services. The provider inventories represent the supply side of the service-delivery equation; the other methods represent the demand side.

Community surveys and client surveys are also logical complements. Surveys of the chronically mentally ill clients cover only that segment of the chronically mentally ill population served. By contrast, the community surveys also cover the unserved segment of the population.

CONCLUSIONS

Prior to applying any of the needs-assessment methods, planners should consider the following questions: What decisions must be made using the needs information (for example, proposed legislation, funding priorities, programmatic or administrative changes)? Who makes these decisions (for example, elected officials, state mental health administrators)? What types of needs information would be most meaningful to these decisionmakers (for example, would elected officials find anecdotal information more or less persuasive than statistical information)? Consideration of such utilization-focused questions in advance of data collection will almost certainly increase the likelihood that the needs-assessment data will be substantial, meaningful, and useful to decisionmakers in planning for services to chronically mentally ill persons.

Planners should be acutely aware of the technical and practical limitations of these methods and should be careful not to misapply them or misrepresent the need. As a case in point, key-informant surveys are not designed to yield quantified estimates of the need for particular services. Only when needs-assessment methods are appropriately chosen, and the results responsibly presented, will they prove useful in improving the delivery of services to the chronically mentally ill.

REFERENCES

Ashbaugh, John; Maryanne Hoff; Valerie Bradley; and Michele Reday. 1980. "Assessing the Needs of the Community Support Program Target Population: Selected Methods for National and State Application." NIMH Contract No. 278-79-0036 (OP), Washington, D.C.: Human Services Research Institute.

Ashbaugh, John; Maryanne Hoff; and Valerie Bradley. 1979. "Community Support Program Needs Assessment Project: A Review of the Findings in the State CSP Reports and Literature." NIMH Contract No. 278-79-0036 (OP). Washington, D.C.: Human Services Research Institute.

Brock, Dwight; Dwight French; and Barry Peyton. 1980. "Small Area Estimation: Empirical Evaluation of Several Estimators for Primary Sampling Units." Section on Survey Research Methods, Proceedings of the American Statistical Association.

Dohrenwend, B.P., and D.L. Crandell. 1970. "Psychiatric Symptoms in Community, Clinic, and Mental Hospital Groups." 126, No. 11 (May): 1611-1621.

Dohrenwend, B.P.; N. Oksenberg; P.E. Shrout; B.S. Dohrenwend; and D. Cook. 1978. "What Psychiatric Screening Scales Measure in the General Population–Part 1: Jerome Frank's Concept of Demoralization." Unpublished manuscript, Columbia University.

Efron, B., and C. Morris. 1973. "Stein's Estimation Rule and Its Competitors–An Empirical Bayes Approach." *Journal of the American Statistical Association* 68, no. 341: 117–30.

———. 1975. "Data Analysis Using Stein's Estimator and Its Generalization." *Journal of the American Statistical Association* 70, no. 350: 311–59.

Fay, R.E., and R.A. Herriot. 1979. "Estimates of Income for Small Places: An Application of James-Stein Procedures to Census Data." *Journal of American Statistical Association* 74: 269–77.

Gonzalez, M.E., and J.E. Waksberg. 1973. "Estimation of the Error of Synthetic Estimates." Paper presented at the first meeting of the International Association of Survey Statisticians, Vienna, Austria.

Gonzalez, M.E., and C. Hoza. 1978. "Small Area Estimation with Application to Unemployment and Housing Estimates." *Journal of American Statistical Association* 73: 7–15.

Hagedorn, Homer. 1977. *Manual on State Mental Health Planning.* Developed Under Contract No. 278–76–0047 (MH), DHEW Publication No. (ADM) 77–473. Rockville, Md.: DHEW Public Health Service, National Institute of Mental Health.

Hollingshead, August B., and Fredrick C. Redlich. 1958. *"Social Class and Mental Illness."* New York: Wiley.

Holzer, C.E.; D.J. Jackson; and D. Tweed. 1981. "Horizontal Synthetic Estimation" *Evaluation and Program Planning* 4: 29–34.

Hughes C.C., Tremblay; R.M. Rapport; and A.H. Leighton. 1960. *People of Cove and Woodlot.* New York: Basic Books.

Human Services Research Institute. 1981. "Estimating the Size and Characteristics of the Chronically Mentally Ill Population of the State and Sub-State Levels." NIMH Contract No. 278–79–0036(OP). Rockville, Md.: The Division of Biometry and Epidemiology, National Institute of Mental Health.

Langner, Thomas S., and Stanley T. Michael. 1963. *Life Stress And Mental Illness, The Midtown Manhattan Study.* Thomas Rennie Series in Social Psychiatry, vol. 2. New York: The Free Press of Glencoe.

Levy, P.S. 1971. "The Use of Mortality Data in Evaluating Synthetic Estimates." In *Proceedings of the Social Statistics Section of the American Statistical Association.* Washington, D.C.: American Statistical Association.

Levy, P.S., and D.K. French. 1977. "Synthetic Estimation of State Health Characteristics Based on the Health Survey Interview." In Vital and Health Statistics, Series 2 no. 75 (October): DHEW Publication No. (HRA) 78–1349, Health Resources Administration. Washington, D.C.: Government Printing Office.

Link, Bruce, and B.P. Dohrenwend. 1980. "Formulation of Hypotheses about the True Prevalence of Demoralization in the United States." In *Mental Illness in the United States,* edited by B.P. Dohrenwend, pp. 114–32. New York: Prager.

Mustian, R. David, and Joel J. See. 1973. "Indicators of Mental Health Needs: An Empirical and Pragmatic Evaluation." *Journal of Health and Social Behavior* 14 (March): 23–27.

Namakata, T,; P.S. Levy; and T.W. O'Rourke. 1975. "Synthetic Estimates of Work Loss Disability for Each State and the District of Columbia." *Pub. Health Rep.* 90:532–38.

National Center for Health Statistics. 1968. *Synthetic State Estimates of Disability.* PHS Publication No. 1759. Public Health Service. Washington, D.C.: Government Printing Office.

Phillips, Derek L., and Kevin J. Clancy. 1970. "Response Biases in Field Studies of Mental Illness." *American Sociological Review* 35(June):503–515.

Purcell, N.J., and L. Kish. 1979. "Estimation for Small Domains." *Biometrics* 35:365–84.

Redick, R.W.; H.F. Goldsmith; and E.L. Unger. *1970 Census Data Used to Indicate Areas with Different Potentials for Mental Health and Related Problems.* Methodology Reports, National Institute of Mental Health, DHEW Publication No. (HSM) 72–9051. Washington, D.C.: Government Printing Office.

Regier, Darrel A. 1979. "Epidemiologic Catchment Area Program Announcement." Rockville, Md.: Division of Biometry and Epidemiology, Center for Epidemiologic Studies, National Institute of Mental Health.

Schaible, W.L.; D.B Brock; and G.A. Schnack. 1977. "An Empirical Comparison of Two Estimators for Small Areas." Paper presented at the Second Annual Data Use Conference of the National Center For Health Statistics, Dallas, Texas.

Schwab, John J.; Roger A. Bell; George J. Warheit; and Ruby B. Schwab. 1979. *Social Order and Mental Health: The Florida Health Study.* New York: Brunner/Mazel.

Segal, S.P., and U. Aviram. 1978. The Mentally Ill in Community-Based Sheltered Care: A Study of Community Care and Social Integration. New York: Wiley-Interscience.

Sigelman, Carol K.; Edward C. Budd; Cynthia L. Spanhel; and Carol J. Schoenrock. 1981. "When in Doubt Say Yes: Acquiescence in Interviews with Mentally Retarded Persons." *American Association on Mental Deficiency.* 19, no. 2 (April):53–58.

Social Security Administration. 1973. *Users' Manual for the 1972 Survey of Disabled and Nondisabled Adults.* ORS Publication No. 026 (3–79). Baltimore, Md.: Division of Disability Studies, Office of Policy and Research Statistics. .

———. 1975. *Users' Manual for the 1974 followup Survey of Disabled and Nondisabled Adults.* SSA Publication No. 13–11725. Baltimore, Md.: Division of Disability Studies, Office of Policy and Research Statistics.

———. 1981. *Users' Manual 1978 Survey of Disability and Work.* SSA Publication No., 13–11732. Baltimore, Md.: Office of Policy and Research Statistics.

Srole, Leo; Thomas S. Langner; Stanley T. Michael; Marvin K. Opler; Thomas A.C. Rennie. 1972. *Mental Health in the Metropolis: The Midtown Manhattan Study.* Thomas A.C. Rennie Series in Social Psychiatry, vol. 1. New York: McGraw Hill.

Tousignant, M.; G. Denis; and R. Lachapelle. 1974. "Some Considerations Concerning the Validity and use of the Health Opinion Survey." *Journal of Health and Social Behavior* 15:241–52.

Trussell, R.E.; J. Elinson; and M.L. Levin. 1956. "Comparisons of Various Methods of Estimating The Prevalence of Chronic Disease in a Community–The Hunterdon County Study." *American Journal of Public Health* 46:173–82.

Turner, J.C. and W.J. TenHoor. 1978. "The NIMH Community Support Program: Pilot Approach to a Needed Social Reform." *Schizophrenia Bulletin* 4, no. 3: 319–48.

Ware, John E., Jr.. 1977. "Effects of Acquiescent Response Set on Patient Satisfaction Ratings." Paper No. P–5676. Santa Monica, California: Rand Corporation.

Warheit, George J.; Joanne M. Buhl; and Roger A. Bell. 1977. *A Critique of Social Indicators Analysis and Key Informants Surveys as Needs Assessment Methods.* Prepared under NIMH grant No. 24740–03. University of Florida, Gainsville.

Warheit, George J.; Roger A. Bell; and John J. Schwab. 1977. *Need Assessment Approaches: Concepts and Methods.* DHEW Publication No. (ADM) 79–472. Rockville, Md.: Public Health Service, National Institute of Mental Health. Rockville, MD.

Weissman, Myrna M.; Jerome K. Myers; and Pamela S. Harding. 1978. "Psychiatric Disorders in a U.S. Urban Community." *American Journal of Psychiatry* 135:459–462.

Wilder, M.. "Current Estimates from the Health Interview Survey 1970." 1973. Vital and Health Statistics, Series 10–72, No. (HRA) 74–1054. National Center for Health Statistics. Washington, D.C.: Government Printing Office.

9 ASSESSING INTERORGANIZATIONAL LINKAGES— Toward A Systems Analysis of Community Support Programs at the Local Level

Joseph P. Morrissey, Ph.D.

Developing a "network of caring" and a sociopolitical base of support for chronically mentally ill persons are major intermediate systems change objectives of the Community Support Program (CSP). Chapter 3 identified these objectives and outlined the expected connection between network development and improvement in services and quality of life for the chronically mentally ill. Chapter 4 raised numerous questions about the plausibility of program logic in this area and the exploratory evaluation work group recommended further study and methodology development. Chapter 5 reported on difficulties in operationalizing variables for assessing systems change in state-level CSP projects. This chapter addresses the research issues involved in assessing interorganizational linkages in a systems analysis of a CSP at the local project level. Its purpose is to offer a conceptual and methodological framework as a guide for further work in this area. The presentation is based on a National Institute of Mental Health (NIMH)-sponsored review of interorganizational research methods (Morrissey, Hall, and Lindsey 1982) and on work in process, evaluating system aspects of a local CSP project in Syracuse, New York (Morrissey and Castellani 1981) and the interorganizational dimensions of mental health services for local jails in forty-two communities across the country (Steadman and Morrissey, 1980).

LOCAL SYSTEM ANALYSES OF CSPs: AN OVERVIEW

A concern with the assessment of community support systems (CSSs) for chronically mentally ill persons transcends the traditional emphases of evaluation research. The focus in most evaluation studies is limited to client and program-level variables. The goals are to ascertain the impact of services on client functioning and to identify which aspects of a treatment program contribute to client outcomes in an efficient and effective way (e.g., Suchman 1967; Campbell and Stanley 1969; Weiss 1972; Riecken and Boruch 1974; Attkisson et al. 1978). When attention shifts from clients and individual programs to "systems of services," a new level of analysis is introduced that requires assessments of transaction processes between a variety of service organizations and their broader social environment. The focus at the system level is on the extent and manner in which diverse and otherwise autonomous organizations act in concert to achieve mutual objectives, and the ways these interorganizational arrangements are affected by factors operating in the broader community, state, and national environment (e.g., Warren et al. 1974; Benson 1975; Turk 1977; Aldrich 1979; Van de Ven and Ferry 1980).

The systems level of analysis is not a substitute for client and program-level evaluations. Each is directed at a different set of issues and relies upon distinctive methodologies and competencies. Relatively speaking, however, research methods are better developed at the client and program levels of assessment. While it is true that a number of conceptual and methodological problems remain to be solved in evaluating the client and program impacts of CSPs (Schulberg 1979; Schulberg and Bromet 1981), most investigators would agree that the procedures for client needs assessment, services utilization, program performance, and even client outcome determinations, are all better elaborated than techniques for assessing the system development and system change objectives of CSP projects. It is important to recognize, nonetheless, that the logic for establishing cause-effect relationships is formally the same in client, program, and system analyses. Moreover, a holistic assessment of the multifaceted goals of CSPs requires an integration of findings from each level of analysis.

Given the imbalance in the respective research traditions, it is not surprising that most of the CSP evaluations conducted to date have focused on clients as opposed to system processes and outcomes (e.g., Lannon 1981). The evaluability and plausibility assessments reviewed in earlier chapters of this book have broached the issues involved in system assessments, but they have concentrated primarily on design and implementation processes at the federal and state levels. These assessments have highlighted the gaps in current knowledge of the ways in which NIMH initiatives can be translated into viable programs for enhancing the quality of life of chronically mentally ill persons in community settings. At present there are no well-documented studies of the antecedents, concomitants, and consequences of CSP systems development and systems change at the local community level. Evaluation of the intermediate and ultimate objectives of CSP projects, therefore, remains as an important agenda for future research.

Only sophisticated research designs and methodologies can unravel the questions raised by the CSP plausibility analysis: Is a service coordination-collaboration approach efficacious in this context? Will changes in the system of care improve the outcome of services and the quality of life of persons with chronic mental disorders? How do CSPs fit into the existing health, mental health, and social service arenas? Can CSP objectives be achieved at the local level without significant new resources from state and federal sources? The remainder of this chapter will illustrate the ways in which the concepts and methods of interorganizational research can be used to address these and related questions concerning the systems development and systems change objectives of CSPs.

Within the past twenty years, interorganizational analysis has emerged as a distinctive field of research occupying an interstitial position between studies of individual organizations and of whole communities. Its focus is on the origins, patterns, and consequences of interaction between complex organizations (Levine and White 1961; Litwak and Hylton 1962; Evan 1966; Warren 1967; Schulberg and Baker 1970; Baker and O'Brien 1971; Benson 1975; Van de Ven 1976). Although spawned within an open-systems theory tradition, interorganizational analysis views as problematic what in many systems formulations is assumed as axiomatic, namely, the tight coupling or high degree of interdependency among community organizations and actors. In other words, "systemness" is conceived of as a variable, and its attribution in any particular domain is a matter to be empirically demonstrated rather than assumed.

The principal topic to which interorganizational analysis has been directed relates to the coordination and integration of human services. The stimulus for this work has been the variety of governmental efforts to overcome the patchwork of fragmented and discontinuous services in the health and welfare field. Sauber (1977:130–31) has characterized this situation in the following terms:

> Gaps in intersystem relationships among health and medical practice, criminal justice, welfare and rehabilitation, education and mental health organizations have long been considered as a major problem and deterrent to effective service delivery. As a result, there is a strong appeal in shifting the focus from the level of the single organization to that of a complex network of agencies and in planning in terms of a community of interorganizational systems of which individual organizations constitute components or subsystems. Applying the term "system" to an organization implies "interdependence" of necessary input and output linkages, but also "independence" in the sense of maintenance of the integrity of system elements through boundary control processes. Human service organizations find themselves entering into relationships and decisions that are aimed at multilevel outcomes. These transactions and resource exchanges must be approached in terms of their relevance to community needs, interorganizational relationships, and intraorganizational requirements for system survival.

In one form or another, the fragmentation of human services has been attributed to the excessive autonomy of service agencies and to their attempts to preserve prerogatives about problem definition, intervention priority, and client disposition (Greenley and Kirk 1973; Levine 1974). From a community-organization perspective, the historic response has been to seek a pattern of coordinated services relying upon mechanisms that would ensure the autonomy of the individual organizations in areas of conflict while at the same time permitting their unified effort in areas of agreement (Litwak and Rothman 1970). The experience with voluntary coordination mechanisms in the

human services field, however, has proven to be rather ineffectu-
al (Warren 1973). More recently, greater attention has been paid
to the managed forms of coordination in concerted decisionmaking among service agencies as well as to the ways conflict can
result from such cooperative actions (Morris and Hirsch-Lescohier 1978). The relative efficacy of these forms, however, has
yet to be carefully documented and their impact to be objective-
ly assessed (Mott 1968; Aldrich 1978).

There has been enough research and informed assessment in
this area to demonstrate that there are costs as well as potential
benefits both from coordination and from autonomy of service
providers (Zald 1969; Landau 1969; Warren 1973; Warren et al.
1974; Agranoff and Mahler 1981). Coordination, for example,
may help to check the narrow professional interests of service
providers while diminishing the problems of duplication and
overlap, but it has associated costs both in terms of reduced autonomy and the salaries of personnel needed to maintain linkages with other organizations. A network of autonomous service
providers, on the other hand, may be more innovative and capable of serving the wants of diverse clients, but it presents obstacles to achieving comprehensive, continuous, and cost-efficient
interventions. Only if these costs and benefits are closely examined and evaluated can effective policies be implemented. Notwithstanding the current emphasis on the integration or
consolidation of mental health and related human services at
the federal, state, and local levels, the implication is that greater
attention must be focused on coordination-integration of what
(tasks, functions), for what or for whom (purposes, beneficiaries,
outcomes), and by what or to what extent (structures, processes)?

These questions are highly salient for the evaluation of CSP
projects. As with the large-scale social programs of the 1960s,
services coordination is one of the program's basic strategies for
promoting system change (Turner and TenHoor 1978). The CSP
projects differ from earlier federal "seed money" initiatives such
as the Community Mental Health Centers (CMHCs) and Model
Cities programs, however, in that massive funding has yet to be
made available as an incentive for interagency collaboration. In
addition, unlike the human services integration projects which
sought to overcome services fragmentation and duplication by

creating umbrella agencies with unified authority structures (e.g., Agranoff and Pattakos 1979), CSPs rely primarily upon voluntary coordination mechanisms to promote resource sharing, joint planning, and continuity of care among otherwise autonomous service providers. The goal is to foster linkages (formal and informal interorganizational relationships) among mental health, medical, rehabilitation, housing, and other agencies which provide psychosocial support services so that a comprehensive network of services for chronically mentally ill persons will be available in communities across the country.

There are three areas of application in which interorganizational research techniques can be used to document the antecedents, concomitants, and consequences of these planned change efforts: (1) system description; (2) system change; and (3) system evaluation. As background for each of these applications, the following section presents an overview of the core concepts and methods of interorganizational research.

CONCEPTS AND METHODS OF INTERORGANIZATIONAL RESEARCH

The interorganizational research field is still at a rather early stage of theoretical and methodological development. The central interests of the field only began to take shape in the early 1960s and most of the key research studies were carried out within the last decade. These studies are informed by a variety of interpretative frameworks such as social exchange, resource dependency, population-ecology, and political economy. Summary expositions of these interorganizational theories and their associated research findings can be found in a number of recent statements (Aldrich 1979; Evan 1978; Pfeffer and Salancik 1978).

Despite this theoretical diversity, there are a core set of generic concepts and research methods which underlie the work in this field. Here we will concentrate on conceptualization and the basic steps involved in conducting research on interorganizational relationships. Other issues of research design will be deferred for consideration as part of the specific applications to CSPs.

Conceptual Framework

The key concepts and variables to be considered in an interorganizational assessment of a local service-delivery system are displayed in Figure 9–1. This conceptual framework is adapted from Van de Ven (1976) and Morrissey, Hall and Lindsey (1982). It arranges many of the major variables that have been used in interorganizational studies into six major clusters: *Environmental Context, Situational Factors, Bases of Interaction, Transaction Structures, Transaction Processes,* and *Outcomes.* Although numerous causal models for linking these clusters of variables into explanatory frameworks have been postulated in the literature, present research findings do not allow for a single best configuration. Consequently, no fixed or unilinear causal sequence is implied by this display. The concepts are clustered only as a heuristic way of identifying the scope and focus of concern in interorganizational research. A detailed profile of the operational definitions and measures associated with each concept is available elsewhere (see Morrissey et al. 1982). Here only a brief synopsis of the content and significance of each cluster will be presented.

The concepts and variables subsumed under TRANSACTION PROCESSES refer to the substantive dimensions of interorganizational relationships. Van de Ven (1976) notes that an interorganizational relationship occurs when two or more organizations transact resources (e.g., money, clients, information, technical services). These *resource flows* create the basis of a social system. The actions of the member agencies become interdependent, and overtime, the organizations take on specialized roles and behavioral expectations emerge regarding the rights and obligations of each member. Resource flows, however, can vary in their significance or *importance* for member agencies. In general, the more important a particular resource transaction is to the goals or interests of each organization, the more frequent or intense is the relationship. In addition, the more intensively a single agency transacts resources with other member organizations, the greater the strategic position or *power* of that agency in the interorganizational system. Power differentials in the flow of resources, in turn, create the basis for both *cooperation* and *conflict* between organizations. To the extent that transactions are mutu-

166   ASSESSING COMMUNITY SUPPORT PROGRAMS

Figure 9–1. Conceptual Framework for Interorganizational Research.

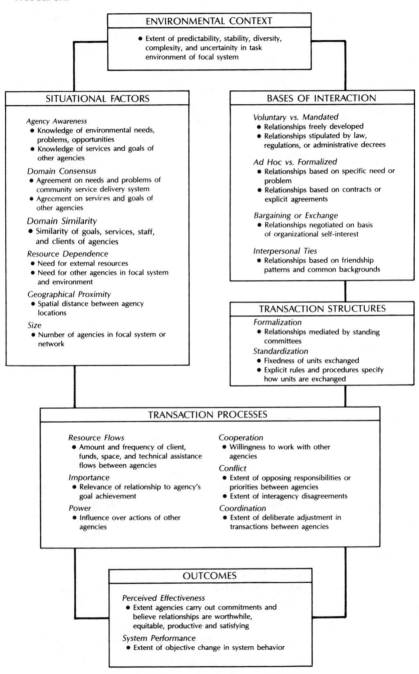

Source: Adapted from Van de Ven (1976) and Morrissey, Hall, and Lindsey (1982)

ally important and the resources sought are relatively scarce, however, organizations may seek a pattern of *coordination* to ensure their unified effort in areas of agreement while allowing for autonomy in areas of competition. To understand the circumstances under which such processes occur, the other variables displayed in Figure 9–1 must be considered.

The SITUATIONAL FACTORS cluster encompasses variables which are often conceptualized as preconditions for interorganizational relationships. While every organization operates in a "field" of other organizations (Warren 1967), *awareness* of this field and of the states of *interdependency* among agencies may vary. In general, awareness provides identification of alternative sources of services and resources, and high levels of awareness are likely to lead to higher levels of interactions (Van de Ven and Ferry 1980). The extent of *domain consensus* or agreement over the role and task differentiation among organizations may affect the degree to which cooperative or conflictual relationships proliferate among interacting organizations (Hall et al. 1977). Likewise, *domain similarity* may facilitate the formation of interorganizational relationships. However, high domain similarity can also increase the potential for territorial disputes and the level of competition for scarce resources. Those agencies which have access to extralocal resources are less dependent on exchanges with other community organizations, and thus they may pursue an independent course of action. *Geographical proximity* and the *size* of the interorganizational system are other situational factors that can influence the patterns and rates of resource transactions.

Interorganizational relationships not only have a content and a situational context; they also arise for some reason or purpose. The BASES OF INTERACTION cluster in Figure 9–1 draws attention to the differential reasons for interagency linkage. Much of the early work in this field viewed transactions between organizations as essentially *voluntary* in nature (Levine and White 1961). More recently, the fact that many interorganizational relationships are *mandated* in federal and state legislative regulations or other administrative-judicial decrees has received increased attention (e.g., Hall et al. 1977). The *ad hoc vs. formalized* nature of these relationships is another basis for differentiating interorganizational relationships. Linkages have an ad hoc basis when there is little or no previous patterning in the relationships among organizations. If an ad hoc situation repeats itself, or if more elements enter the relationships among the agencies involved, more formalized bases for a continued relationship (such as explicit agreements or contracts) will often develop. Another distinct dimension is the *interpersonal* basis of these relationships. In some circumstances, friendship ties may override other bases for forming interagency linkages (Galaskiewicz and Shatin 1981).

The TRANSACTION STRUCTURES cluster encompasses variables that define the administrative arrangements established to define the role relationships among member agencies (Van de Ven 1976). Oftentimes, *formalization* and *standardization* of relationships are treated as synonymous. In Figure 9–1 a distinction is drawn, however, between the rules and procedures governing the relationship and whether or not a third agency or committee mediates the transactions between member organizations. The former concept references the degree of standardization while the latter indexes the extent of formalization. If organizations agree to exchange uniform or homogeneous types of clients in a routine manner, for example, high standardization is present. To the extent that resource transactions are variable or heterogeneous, and handled on a case-by-case basis, then low standardization would be present. High formalization would be exemplified by the United Fund, Welfare Boards, and other interagency committees that serve mediating or coordinating functions for member agencies. Both types of structural arrangements are likely to occur to the extent that relationships are persistent and well defined. In combination with transaction process variables, these structural dimensions provide an interorganizational action system with a unit character or identity that is distinct from the behaviors of the individual member organizations when each is considered in isolation from the others.

In addition to the structure, process, and situational dimensions of a focal interorganizational system, one must consider its relationships to the broader social environment in which it operates. The ENVIRONMENTAL CONTEXT cluster in Figure 9–1 refers to these external influences which can exert a decisive impact on interorganizational relationships in any local service-delivery system. Often, the environment is conceptualized in a residual way as encompassing a variety of technological, legal, political, economic, demographic, ecological, and cultural conditions which influence organizational behavior (Hall 1977). Increasingly, however, researchers have examined a number of dimensional properties of the environment which create opportunities as well as constraints on interorganizational relationships (Aldrich 1979). These dimensions include the *predictability, stability, diversity, complexity,* and *uncertainty* of extrasystem events and processes. These different states of the environment can influence the probability and type of linkage formation and, once established, the likelihood of their persistence or deterioration. Changes in funding streams or the availability of external resources through new governmental appropriations or cutbacks, for example, can markedly alter the preconditions and incentives for interorganizational coordination.

The remaining group of variables displayed in Figure 9–1 is associated with the OUTCOMES cluster. The results or outcomes of interorganizational relationships can be conceptualized in two general ways. The first relates to the subjective evaluations of member-agency representatives and the second refers to more objective changes in the system of relationships among the interacting agencies. Van de Ven and Ferry (1981) suggest that *perceived effectiveness* can be indexed by the extent to which member organizations carry out their commitments and the degree to which relationships are viewed as productive, worthwhile, and satisfying. Assessments of *system performance,* in turn, depend upon the particular goals and objectives of the interorganizational network. For human service delivery systems, performance indices might encompass variables such as continuity of care, cost efficiency, accessibility, and equity of service delivery (Keppler-Seid et al. 1980; Morrissey et al. 1982). Over time, the outcomes of interorganizational behavior (both positive and negative) create feedback loops that can influence the structure, process, and situational aspects of system activity as well as the states of its environmental context.

Research Methods

While there are several useful treatises on research design considerations in organizational research (e.g., Barton 1961; Price 1972;

Haas and Drabek, 1973), there are few guides for interorganizational studies. Many of the measurement and analysis conventions in this field remain embedded in journals and research monographs. Only recently have investigators begun to address the methodological issues in interorganizational research (e.g., Aldrich and Whetten 1981; Van de Ven and Ferry 1980; Whetten 1981; Morrissey et al. 1982). Here attention will focus on four issues basic to any interorganizational study plan: (1) bounding the system, (2) choosing respondents, (3) collecting the data, and (4) analyzing the results. A review of options and procedures in each area will highlight the interorganizational research process and provide a backdrop for a discussion of CSP applications.

Bounding the System   The first decision that confronts any investigator seeking to study interorganizational relationships is specification of the focal system of analysis. The issue here is to determine criteria for inclusion or exclusion of community organizations from the study universe. While at first this might seem a rather straightforward task, in practice, a number of complexities arise. The logic of interorganizational systems analysis requires enumeration of all organizations that participate in or influence the flow of resources in a given action arena, whether it is the corporate banking structure of a community, a manpower-training program, or a community mental health system. The task is to gather information on the relationships between these organizations according to the structure, process, and outcome framework identified above. Clearly, if irrelevant organizations are included in the study universe, the burdens of data collection and analysis will be excessive on both respondents and the research staff. A far more costly error, however, is to inadvertently exclude one or more agencies that play a key role in the interorganizational system. In this case, information about the structure and processes of resource flows will be incomplete and the investigator runs the risk of drawing inferences and recommendations that are unduly trivial or misleading.

Laumann, Galaskiewicz, and Marsden (1978), in a recent review of the research literature, found that inclusion rules have for the most part been only implicitly stated in published reports. Most investigators seem to rely on a functional and/or geographic delimitation of a relevant population or system of organizations.

The first criterion serves to restrict the set of organizations to those that are functionally interdependent or those that share a common or collective goal. The second criterion uses the geographical community to define system or network boundaries. Even within these broad limits, problems may arise especially regarding extralocal agencies, which, while not "present" in the community, may exert considerable influence as a result of their control over resource inputs to the local system.

In practice, the ease with which a system is bounded depends on prior familiarity with the agencies and actors in the local community. In those cases where a small number of agencies are known to be the key actors in an action arena, system specification can proceed fairly easily. In other situations, where the investigator is less familiar with the community, exploratory fieldwork and interviews with key informants can help to bound the system.

In an ongoing study of local jail-mental health agency linkages, for example, the author and his colleagues were able to specify the network of interest in each of forty two communities from around the country through on-site interviews with key informants. These visits were preceded by telephone contacts with the local sheriff or jail administrator to learn about the interorganizational composition of his mental health service program. On-site interviews then explored the nature and scope of each linkage, the presence and role of other provider agencies, the most appropriate respondent from each agency or subunit, and the other logistic questions which are crucial in data collection (see below). In many ways, "bounding the system" can become a miniature research project in its own right. Attention to detail at this point will have payoffs at each successive stage of the study.

Choosing Respondents   Unlike in other areas of social science research, it is exceedingly difficult to conduct direct observational studies of interorganizational relationships. While observational methods might be used to study interactions between two or three agencies, this technique becomes totally impractical for primary data collection when a large number of organizations are involved in the system or if multiple sites are included in the study. Consequently, survey research procedures are usually employed in interorganizational studies.

The reliance on survey research methods immediately raises the issue of choosing respondents as sources of information. The selection process is akin to the boundary-specification problem discussed above but the task here is to identify knowledgeable respondents from each of the organizations included in the study universe. The respondent-specification problem involves two interrelated tasks. The first is to determine whether each organization can be treated as a single entity or whether otherwise holistic organizations should be disaggregated into functional subunits which are then treated in the data collection and analysis as if they were discrete organizations. The second task is to identify one or more persons from each organization to serve as respondents in the data collection process.

Here again, explicit or widely accepted criteria are lacking. Disaggregation would appear to make sense for large, decentralized organizations which are differentiated into distinct subunits, such as the inpatient and outpatient units of a CMHC or a state mental hospital. In these types of organizations the subunits tend to be rather functionally autonomous (often with separate staff and budgets) and linked with different agencies in the community. Given the variability that would likely result on the structure, process, and outcome dimensions of each unit's interorganizational relationships, it would be difficult and possibly misleading to assign a single score or value to the overall organization. For smaller and less differentiated organizations, the unitary approach would be more appropriate.

Although multiperson samples have been used in interorganizational research (e.g., Aiken and Hage 1967; Hall et al. 1977), the far more common approach has been to select a single key informant from each organization or subunit. Often the person selected is the agency director. While it is much easier to design and collect data from an individual key informant than from a sample of respondents, the choice of a strategy should be based on conceptual as well as logistical considerations. An agency director, for example, might be a knowledgeable respondent for budgetary and policy aspects of an agency's relations with other organizations but a poor source of information on client flow or day-to-day transactions involving direct services. Some investigators attempt to compensate for differential respondent knowledge by selecting the key "boundary spanner" or person who is most directly involved in transactions with other organizations (Aldrich and Herker 1977). In some cases this position might be located at the executive level of the organization; more often it would be located at the technical or direct-service level. In large service organizations where no single respondent is familiar with the full range of interorganizational transactions, a multiple respondent sampling strategy would be indicated.

Collecting the Data   The primary data collection instruments employed in interorganizational studies are interviews and questionnaires. While many of the early studies in this field relied upon qualitative techniques and open-ended questions, there is a growing convergence on quantitative measures of the core concepts displayed in Figure 9–1. A detailed profile of these measures has recently been compiled by Morrissey, Hall and Lindsey (1982). Another useful source of measures and research schedules can be found in Van de Ven and Ferry (1980). Many of the recent journal articles in this field contain methodological appendixes which often present the survey items used to measure dimensions of interorganizational relations.

The logic of the data-collection process is to have each respondent answer questions concerning the relationships between his organization or subunit and each of the other agencies included in the study. The question content focuses on one or another aspect of the environment-structure-process-outcome dimensions listed in Figure 9–1. By obtaining information on each pairwise or dyadic relationship in the focal system or universe of agencies, the resultant data can be configured into systemwide indicators as described later in this chapter.

The choice of interviews or self-administered questionnaires depends on several considerations. One obvious constraint is the size of the research budget. Multirespondent samples, especially using interviews in a large number of organizations, are time consuming and expensive. A limited budget on a short time-frame dictates a less labor-intensive data collection strategy, such as key-informant interviews or questionnaires. Another consideration is the anticipated mindset of the respondent. One advantage of "in person" interviews is that the investigator can better explain the context of the study to the respondent and help to draw out the idea of an "interorganizational system" which otherwise might be foreign in the day-to-day conceptualizations of the respondent. To the extent that the context can be clearly stated in a cover letter and a small number of organizations are included in the study universe, a self-administered questionnaire would be more cost efficient. One compromise strategy which the author and his colleagues have used with success is to conduct a brief orientation interview with each respondent and then leave a questionnaire to be subsequently completed and mailed back.

Another consideration is respondent burden and the degree of access researchers have to each organization in the study universe. While an agency director might be willing to participate in a study involving a single interview, for example, his tolerance may rapidly dissipate in the face of multiple interviews or questionnaire administrations with agency staff. As in any survey research project, success in implementing a research design is highly correlated with time spent enlisting the interest and cooperation of respondents.

In addition to interviews and questionnaires, other more objective types of data can be obtained from agency reports, public documents, and management information systems. These sources are especially useful for quantitative data on agency caseloads, budgets, legal requirements, and staffing patterns. Staff logs have also been used to secure more precise information on the frequency and nature of interagency contacts (e.g., Rieker, Horan, and Morrissey 1976; Flaherty, Barry, and Swift 1978). The advantage of obtaining objective as well as subjective data is the resultant opportunity to cross-validate the information collected. Findings can be greatly strengthened when data collected by different means can be shown to reinforce a particular conclusion.

Analyzing the Results   In general, the choice of analytical procedures depends upon the particular unit of analysis chosen for study. In some cases, investigators focus on pairwise relationships only, in other cases a particular focal agency is chosen for study and the analysis centers on its relationships with other members of its organization-set. In a full network study, analysis is directed at the structure and processes of the relationships between all organizations in the collectivity or system of interest. In pairwise and organization-set studies, correlation and regression procedures are typically employed to establish patterns of covariation between structure, process, and outcome variables. Network-level studies typically involve a more complex analysis process. Since the raw data are based on all pairwise relations among network members, the first step in data analysis is to develop a simultaneous configuration of these relationships to represent the network as a relational system. This is usually accomplished by sociometric or other statistical clustering procedures (Burt 1980). Once the data have been transformed into network-level indices, the analysis can proceed with the use of regression and other multivariate statistical procedures.

The network model is most germane to system analyses of CSP projects. The goals of these projects are to create a system, or coordinated network, of services for the chronically mentally ill among community mental health, welfare, and psychosocial rehabilitation agencies. The specific ways in which the concepts and methods of interorganizational research can be applied to the assessment of these projects is considered in the remainder of this chapter. These applications will be discussed in relation to system description, system change, and system evaluation.

SYSTEM DESCRIPTION

The program model described in Chapter 3 identifies ten core services or functions as the basis of a comprehensive CSS for chronically mentally ill persons. These component elements encompass client identification and outreach, sustenance and health-welfare entitlements, mental health care, 24-hour crisis-stabilization assistance, comprehensive psychosocial services, rehabilitative and supportive housing options, family and community backup services, mobilization of natural support systems, client advocacy and rights assurances, and case management services. In addition, the model calls for a *core service agency* to assume the lead role in helping severely mentally disabled people to improve their lives in the community.

Unlike earlier NIMH initiatives, such as the CMHCs, a standard national template or service configuration was not superimposed on these CSS elements. Rather, it was assumed from the outset that the size of the target population, the availability of service elements, and the optimal configuration of service providers would vary widely in different communities. Consequently, flexibility in adapting the general prescriptions and service requirements of the CSS model to the realities of programming in each local context was permitted and encouraged. In practice, this type of latitude results in a wide range of CSS programs that share a set of common objectives but differ in the administrative and interorganizational mechanisms used for their accomplishment.

The first application of interorganizational analysis to CSS programs involves system description—uncovering and documenting the nature of the interagency linkages which constitute the local system of services. For ease of presentation, the following discussion will speak in terms of a single site. The principles involved in the study of a single program are readily generalized to comparative, multisite studies. Here the logic of system description will be outlined schematically in three steps: (1) identifying the CSS, (2) documenting resource and information flows, and (3) analyzing the care-giving system.

Identifying the CSS

One of the first steps involved in planning for the development of a CSS is to inventory existing community agencies to determine which of the ten service components are already available, which services are available but need to be expanded, and which are unavailable and need to be newly created. This task is akin to a needs-assessment survey (see Chapter 8) with the focus on providers rather than clients. Figure 9–2 illustrates a schema for cross-classifying information on CSS components by service providers using a hypothetical set of agencies. At this stage, the goal is to conduct an exhaustive inventory of community agencies to identify whether, and in what ways, they are involved in meeting the needs of chronically mentally ill persons. Relevant information might be obtained from community-service directories, planning-agency fact-finding reports, or a first-hand survey of each agency.

Arraying information in this way provides a summary overview of existing service providers, the nature and extent of their involvement in CSS service functions, and any gaps or deficiencies to be overcome as part of a system development or system change strategy. Such an inventory is also useful in those settings where a CSS program has already been mounted prior to the start of research. In the latter instance, this chart would help to identify the roles of each agency in the overall CSS project.

From a research point of view, information of this sort is essential for bounding the system or network of agencies to be included in the study. In communities of even moderate size, the number of agencies included can be quite large. Ongoing research on the NIMH-CSP demonstration project in Syracuse (New York), for example, has identified forty agencies that are related in one way or another to serving the chronically mentally ill. Moreover, the Hutchings Psychiatric Center (state hospital), which serves as the core service agency, was differentiated into twenty seven distinct functional subunits in order to examine the differential involvement of each unit with CSS services and other organizations in the Syracuse metropolitan area. In this way a

Figure 9–2. Assessing Resources for Community Support Systems.

CSS COMPONENTS \ COMMUNITY SERVICE AGENCIES	Apex General Hospital	Central State Hospital	Jonesville CMHC	County Social Services	County Vocational Rehab.	Fairview Adult Residence	Phoenix Social Club	United Sheltered Workshop	Visiting Nurses Association
Identification & Outreach									
Sustenance & Entitlement									
Mental Health Care									
24-Hour Crisis Assistance									
Psychological Services									
Rehab. & Supportive Housing									
Family & Community Backup									
Natural Support Mobilization									
Grievances & Clients Rights									
Case Management									

total of sixty-seven "organizations" were included in the study universe.

It is difficult to gather information on all of the variables displayed in Figure 9–1 from agencies in a network of this size. The reason is that each respondent would be asked to profile the relationships between his or her agency and each of sixty-six other organizations. Even with a large number of "blanks" (signifying no working relationship) the task would be tedious and time consuming, with respondent attrition a likely result. One approach which reduces the task to manageable proportions is to request each respondent to select the five most important agencies from a list containing all organizations of interest. This approach has been utilized successfully by Van de Ven and his colleagues in studies of early childhood development agencies in Texas (Van de Ven et al. 1979; Van de Ven and Ferry 1980). It was also followed in the Syracuse CSP study and in a separate study by Townsend (1980) of the Schenectady (New York) CSP project. The validity of this approach rests on the assumption that the primary relationships of each agency will be identified and that the structure of the overall network can be derived from the pattern of choices among all of the agencies.

Documenting Resource and Information Flows

Once the range of agencies and their involvement in CSS services has been identified, the next step is to assess the pattern of interagency resource and information flow. Resource flows, it will be recalled from Figure 9–1, are the units of value transacted between agencies (e.g., money, clients, personnel, equipment and space, technical assistance). Information flows are communications about these transactions (e.g., written reports and letters, phone calls, face-to-face discussions, group or committee meetings). As Van de Ven (1976) notes, resource and information flows are the major processes within interorganizational relationships; without them a social action system would cease to exist. Thus, an effort to document the extent or degree of "systemness" among a network of agencies must start with the question, "Who does what with whom, and why?"

On the basis of data gathered by the survey research and related procedures described earlier, information on the direction and volume of resource flows can be arranged in a series of interaction matrices (Figure 9-3). These matrices are analogous to sociometric networks at the interpersonal level (Davis 1970) and input-output tables in economics (Hutchinson and Krause 1969; Caplow and Finsterbusch 1968; Burgess et al. 1974). Agencies "sending" resources are arrayed on one axis and agencies "receiving" resources are arrayed on the other. Cell entries would represent the number, volume, dollar value, and so forth, of resources transacted between each agency pair. A separate matrix can be created in this manner for each distinct type of resource transaction. Similarly, other matrices can be created for each type of information flow.

By comparing cell entries *within* each matrix a variety of indices of interagency resource and information flow can be derived. The number of times one agency is chosen by the other organizations, for example, provides an index of its perceived importance or centrality in the network. Reciprocated (two-way flow) and unreciprocated (one-way flow) relationships can also be identified. Moreover, by computing simple ratios of resources sent to resources received, quantitative indices of the degrees of resource interdependency can be obtained for each agency and for the network as a whole (Caplow and Finsterbusch 1968).

Comparisons *between* matrices yield insights into the division of labor and patterning of relationships among CSS agencies. It would be possible, for example, to determine the extent of correspondence between each type of resource transaction (e.g., does the direction and volume of client referrals follow the direction and volume of funding flow?) and the extent of correspondence between each type of information transaction (e.g., does the direction and volume of informal communications overlap formal communications?). More importantly, from the viewpoint of system coordination, one could determine the extent to which resource and information flows overlap in a balanced fashion. The existence of subnetworks or interagency coalitions could also be identified by locating agencies which differ in degrees of linkage, ranging from tightly-coupled (high volume, multiple ties) to loosely coupled (low volume, single ties) clusters in the overall network (e.g., Van de Ven et al. 1979).

Figure 9-3.   Interaction Matrices for CSS Resource and Information Flows.

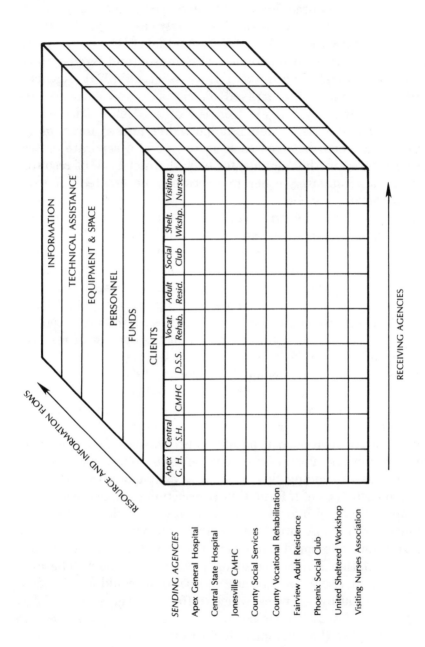

Analyzing the Care-Giving System

Although the illustrations presented above are based solely on re-
source-and-information-flow data, similar configurations can be
developed from data on patterns of interagency cooperation, conflict, coordination, and the other relational variables identified in
Figure 9–1. Computer-based analysis techniques simplify the ma-
nipulation and comparison of large interaction matrices (Burt
1980). These techniques can also generate graphic displays of the
relationships between agencies in the network analogous to the
one depicted in Figure 9–4. Agencies are located in these relational maps as a function of the magnitude of their transactions such
that, the greater the interaction, the closer their spatial location
(see Rieker et al. 1976). The advantage of these "orgiograms"
(Hall 1977) is that they summarize a large volume of data in an
intuitively appealing way.

In conjunction with descriptive data on the characteristics of
individual agencies, these relational maps can be used to analyze

Figure 9–4. Mapping Interorganizational Relationships of
Community Support System Agencies.

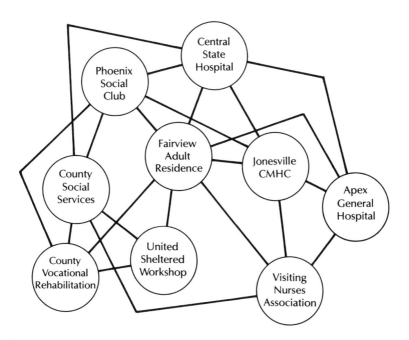

the structure and processes at work in the care-giving system. A number of questions can be addressed at this stage of the analysis: Does the CSS network display a high level of systemness as indicated by a structure of resource flows connecting the component agencies, frequent patterns of communication and cooperative activities, and mechanisms for resolving conflicts when they arise? What about the degree of role clarity among the agencies? Do the data indicate the presence of a mutually agreed-upon division of labor? Are there high levels of domain consensus among the agencies? Is there a strong commitment to developing and coordinating services for chronic mental patients? Answers to these questions can also help to identify service gaps and barriers to the system change goals of the CSS program.

In summary, at the descriptive level, interorganizational research techniques provide a way of obtaining baseline information or a "snapshot" view of CSS relationships at one point in time. Periodic resurveys of the network (e.g., on an annual basis) would provide a data base for monitoring changes in the system of services over time. The format of data collection and analysis at each successive time period would follow the schema presented above. By comparing the state of the system at different time points, inferences can be derived about progress toward goal attainment, increases in system effectiveness, and higher levels of system performance. A number of key issues about system change and evaluation should be addressed in these longitudinal analyses. These issues are the focus of the next section.

SYSTEM CHANGE AND SYSTEM EVALUATION

In considering the extension of the above research framework to assessments of system change and system evaluation, we come full circle to the plausibility issues raised in Chapter 4. There it was noted that the causal links postulated to exist between multiple system changes, services improvement, and client-related outcomes remain to be empirically demonstrated. A full consideration of the kinds of research designs that are needed to test these causal sequences is beyond the scope of this chapter. Here several issues will be identified as an organizing focus for further study. These issues will be discussed in relation to three broad questions which lie at the heart of the CSP initiative. First, do the interorganizational relationships among CSP agencies move toward a well-coordinated system of services? Second, does increased coordination lead to improvements in system performance? And third, do changes in system performance enhance the quality of life for chronically mentally ill persons? Figure 9–5, which is adapted from Redburn (1977), displays these causal connections in a schematic way and it will be used in the following discussion to highlight the issues involved.

In system change analyses, interest shifts from the state of preintervention relationships among CSP agencies to their configuration at one or more subsequent time periods. At issue is the

Figure 9–5.   Relationships Between Structural Changes, System Performance, and Quality of Life.

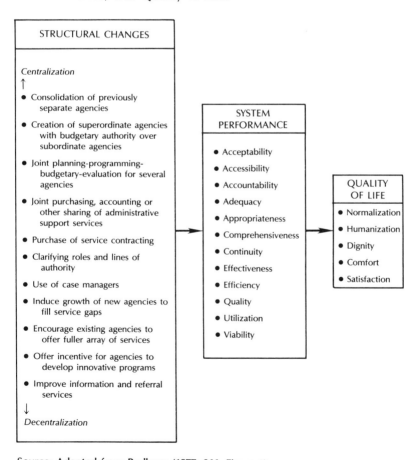

STRUCTURAL CHANGES

Centralization
↑
● Consolidation of previously separate agencies

● Creation of superordinate agencies with budgetary authority over subordinate agencies

● Joint planning-programming-budgetary-evaluation for several agencies

● Joint purchasing, accounting or other sharing of administrative support services

● Purchase of service contracting

● Clarifying roles and lines of authority

● Use of case managers

● Induce growth of new agencies to fill service gaps

● Encourage existing agencies to offer fuller array of services

● Offer incentive for agencies to develop innovative programs

● Improve information and referral services
↓
Decentralization

SYSTEM PERFORMANCE

● Acceptability
● Accessibility
● Accountability
● Adequacy
● Appropriateness
● Comprehensiveness
● Continuity
● Effectiveness
● Efficiency
● Quality
● Utilization
● Viability

QUALITY OF LIFE

● Normalization
● Humanization
● Dignity
● Comfort
● Satisfaction

Source: Adapted from Redburn (1977: 266, Figure 1).

extent to which relationships have changed to a more coordinated or integrated state and the nature of obstacles that continue to block the achievement of CSP goals.

In attempting to measure system change at the local level, much confusion and circular reasoning can be avoided by distinguishing between coordination as a set of administrative techniques or structural arrangements on the one hand, and coordination as a characteristic of services or their manner of delivery on the other (Redburn 1977). In Figure 9–5, these distinct meanings of the term are labeled *structural changes* and *system performance,* respectively. By conceptualizing and measuring the two sets of phenomena separately, the possible causal connections between them can be investigated.

As suggested in Figure 9–5, a variety of administrative mechanisms might be used to induce structural change, ranging from highly centralized to highly decentralized options (Aldrich 1978; Morris and Hirsch-Lescohier 1978). Similarly, the performance of the system can be indexed by a number of factors ranging from accessibility to fiscal viability. There is no necessary reason to expect that each type of structural change will have a uniform and positive impact on each system performance indicator. Nor is there reason to anticipate that maximizing one performance indicator will maximize the others. As Redburn (1977:265) notes, for example, "... increasing access to services may overload the system—reducing efficiency or effectiveness." Viewed in this way, it then becomes possible to explore the causal relationships between the introduction of various structural changes and a change in the way the service system performs.

The CSP model embodies a particular configuration of these structural changes (voluntary coordination using a core service agency and case-management procedures) tending toward a decentralized intervention strategy. This model assumes that there is a pattern of covariation between system-performance criteria and these structural changes. By profiling the interorganizational dimensions of these structural changes, the resultant measures can be used as a set of "independent" or predictor variables to explain variations in performance outcomes or "dependent" variables. To the extent that CSPs in different communities utilize different combinations of these structural interventions, comparative multisite studies could address the issue as to the relative impact of each combination on performance outcomes, such as accessibility, continuity and cost efficiency. Figure 9–5 also suggests that there are alternative models of structural change oriented toward more-centralized intervention strategies. To the extent that empirical cases of these alternative strategies could be included in the assessment, research studies could then be designed to test the relative impact of alternative approaches on system performance.

Short of these model comparisons, useful information about system change can be obtained from assessments of CSP sites with different core service agencies. The initial round of CSP demonstration sites, for example, contained a range of core service agencies such as CMHCs, state mental hospitals, and nonprofit multiservice agencies. There is evidence to suggest that program auspices does make a difference in the way mental health services are delivered to clients (e.g., Brissenden and Lennard 1970). To the extent that comparative studies of CSPs demonstrate that one type of core service agency is associated with more optimal system performance, the data would provide insights into the behavior of interorganizational service-delivery systems and the ways in which these systems can be modified to meet the needs of chronically mentally ill persons.

Other system performance indices that should be monitored in system-change assessments include resource utilization and fiscal visibility. One of the intermediate system-change goals of CSP is to include a greater allocation of community mental health funds to the long term care of the chronically mentally ill and to access mainstream funding from the larger health and social welfare systems. It would be useful in these regards to determine whether one type of CSP administrative model is more effective in realizing these goals. It may also be important to document the manner in which achieving one goal or one set of goals may hinder or even block the achievement of other goals. Another crucial factor to consider is the influence of state and federal policies. The most significant determinants of resource adequacy and program viability at the local level may well reside at higher governmental levels. With the advent of block-grant funding for human services, the political process at the state level will undoubtedly shape what can and cannot be accomplished on the local community level.

The ultimate issues for CSP assessment concern the causal links between system performance and the quality of life of persons with chronic mental disabilities (Figure 9–5). As noted in a recent monograph prepared by the New York State Office of Mental Health's Bureau of Community Support Systems (NYSOMH, 1980), quality of life may well be the most appropriate outcome measure of CSP interventions. Here the issue is the extent to which improvements in system performance actually translate into humane, dignified, and satisfying conditions of community living for chronically disabled clients.

The evaluation of these outcomes necessitates the integration of system, program, and client-level data. Studies that encompass each set of variables are relatively rare in the health and welfare field. At present, there is little solid evidence to demonstrate that organization-level independent variables predict to client-level dependent variables. In one of the few efforts to demonstrate such a relationship, Ernest Gruenberg has argued that "organization makes the difference," at least in terms of the clinical care of the chronically mentally ill (Gruenberg and Huxley 1970:432). The extension and updating of this finding relative to the quality of life associated with CSP interventions clearly remains as a challenge for further research.

Great care must be exercised in defining and measuring quality-of-life indicators as ultimate success-failure criteria for CSP interventions. Richard Lamb (1981) has noted, for example, that expectations for chronically mentally ill persons expressed in such terms as "helping them become part of the mainstream of our society" and "normalization" are unrealistic save for a minority of this population. Much more appropriate goals for the majority of these people involve living lives of dignity with a reasonable amount of comfort in the community. To the extent that these latter goals are attained, Lamb and others would argue that deinstitutionalization and CSP initiatives will have accomplished a tremendous amount.

CONCLUSIONS

This chapter has outlined an approach to systems analysis of CSPs at the local community level. Drawing upon the concepts and methods of interorganizational research, three areas of application were identified: system description, system change, and system evaluation. These applications illustrate the ways in which interorganizational analysis can be used to document and assess the goals of the CSP initiative as well as other models of service delivery that might be mounted in the years ahead. Although the long-term viability of CSPs in an era of fiscal conservatism remains very much in doubt, it is certain that the humane care of chronically mentally ill persons will remain a societal responsibility for the foreseeable future. Whatever service configuration is ultimately selected as the preferred model, it surely will be multiorganizational in auspices and performance. To that extent, the ideas developed in this chapter concerning the structure and dynamics of interorganizational relationships will continue to be important guides for program monitoring and evaluation.

In closing, it is crucial to sound a cautionary note concerning what can be expected from a strategy that relies exclusively on "fixing the bureaucracy" as the solution to the problems of chronic mental illness in the community. No amount of tinkering with interorganizational relationships will, in and of itself, lead to an improved quality of life for the chronically mentally ill. Lamb (1981:107) has recently argued that "this solution ... holds out the hope that we can improve conditions for the severely mentally ill at very little added cost and thereby provides a rationalization for appropriating minimal funds for these chronically underserved patients." As noted in Chapter 4, the plausibility analysis of CSP clearly acknowledged that current resource allocations are inadequate to achieve the program's broad range of objectives on a national basis. It is only from the combination of adequate resources with effective organizational arrangements that we can reasonably expect these objectives to be attained.

REFERENCES

Agranoff, R., and J. Mahler. 1981. "Mental Health Systems and the Coordination of Services." In *Community Mental Health: A Sourcebook for Professionals and Advisory Board Members,* edited by W. Silverman, pp. 290–310. New York: Praeger.

Agranoff, R., and A. Pattakos. 1979."Dimensions of Services Integration: Service Delivery, Program Linkages, Policy Management, Organizational Structure." DHEW Publication No. 02-76-130. *Human*

Service Monograph Series 13, Project Share. Washington, D.C.: Government Printing Office.

Aiken, M., and J. Hage. 1968. "Organizational Interdependence and Interorganizational Structure." *American Sociological Review* 33(December):912–30.

Aldrich, H. 1978. "Centralization Versus Decentralization in the Design of Human Service Delivery Systems: A Response to Gouldner's Lament." In *The Management of Human Services,* edited by R. Sarri and Y. Hassenfeld, pp. 51–79. New York: Columbia University Press.

————. 1979. *Organizations and Environments.* Englewood Cliffs, N.J: Prentice-Hall.

Aldrich, H., and D. Herker. 1977. "Boundary Spanning Roles and Organization Structure." *Academy of Management Review* (April):217–30.

Aldrich, H., and D. Whetten. 1981. "Organization-Sets, Action-Sets, and Networks: Making the Most of Simplicity." In *Handbook of Organizational Design,* Vol. 1., edited by P. Nystrom and W. Starbuck, pp. 385–408. New York: Oxford University Press.

Attkisson, C.: W. Hargreaves; M. Horowitz; and J. Sorenson, eds. 1978. *Evaluation of Human Service Programs.* New York: Academic Press.

Baker, F., and G. O'Brien. 1971. "Intersystems Relations and Coordination of Human Service Organizations." *American Journal of Public Health* 61:130–37.

Barton, A. 1961. *Organizational Measurement and Its Bearing on the Study of College Environments.* New York: College Entrance Examination Board.

Benson, J.K. 1975. "The Interorganizational Network as a Political Economy." *Administrative Science Quarterly* 20(June):229–49.

Brissenden, R., and H. Lennard. 1970. "Organization of Mental Health Services and Its Effect on the Treatment Career of the Patient." *Mental Hygiene* 54(July):416–20.

Burgess, J.; R. Nelson: and R. Walhaus. 1974. "Network Analysis as a Method for the Evaluation of Service Delivery Systems." *Community Mental Health Journal* 10:337–44.

Burt, R. 1980. "Models of Network Structure." *Annual Review of Sociology* 6:79–141.

Campbell, D., and J. Stanley. 1969. *Experimental and Quasi-Experimental Designs for Research.* Chicago: Rand McNally.

Caplow, T., and K. Finsterbusch. 1968. "France and Other Countries: A Study of International Interaction." *Journal of Conflict Resolution* 12(March):1–15.

Davis, J. 1970. "Clustering and Hierarchy in Interpersonal Relations." *American Sociological Review* 35:843–52.

Evan, W. 1966. "The Organization-Set: Toward a Theory of Interorganizational Relations." In *Approachs to Organizational Design,* edited by J. Thompson, pp. 175–90. Pittsburgh, Pa.: University of Pittsburgh Press.

———. 1978. *Interorganizational Relations.* Philadelphia, Pa.: University of Pennsylvania Press.

Flaherty, E.; E. Barry; and M. Swift. 1978. "Use of an Unobtrusive Measure for the Evaluation of Interagency Coordination." *Evaluation Quarterly* 2(May):261–73.

Galaskiewicz, J., and D. Shatin. 1981. "Leadership and Networking Among Neighborhood Human Service Organizations." *Administrative Science Quarterly* 26(September):434–48.

Greenley, J., and S. Kirk. 1973. "Organizational Characteristics of Agencies and the Distribution of Services to Applicants." *Journal of Health and Social Behavior* 14:70–79.

Gruenberg, E., and J. Huxley. 1970. "Mental Health Services Can be Organized to Prevent Chronic Disability." *Community Mental Health Journal* 6:431–36.

Haas, J., and T. Drabek. 1973. *Complex Organizations: A Sociological Perspective.* New York: MacMillan.

Hall, R. 1977. *Organizations: Structure and Process,* 2nd Edition. Englewood-Cliffs, N.J.: Prentice-Hall.

Hall, R.; J. Clark; P. Giordano; and P. Johnson. 1977. "Patterns of Interorganizational Relationships." *Administrative Science Quarterly* 22(September):457–74.

Halpert, H. 1970. "Models for the Application of Systems Analysis to the Delivery of Mental Health Services." In *Community Psychology and Community Mental Health,* edited by P. Cook, pp. 237–65. San Francisco, Calif.: Holden-Day.

Hutchinson, B., and E. Krause. 1969. "Systems Analysis and Mental Health Services." *Community Mental Health Journal* 5:29–45

Keppler-Seid, H.; C. Windle; and J. R. Woy. 1980. "Performance Measures for Mental Health Programs: Something Better, Something Worse, or More of the Same?" *Community Mental Health Journal* 16(Fall):217–34.

Lamb, H.R. 1981. "What Did We Really Expect From Deinstitutionalization." *Hospital and Community Psychiatry* 32(February):105–9.

Landau, M. 1969. "Redundancy, Rationality, and the Problem of Duplication and Overlap." *Public Administration Review* 29(July–August):346–58.

Lannon, P. 1981. *Evaluation of the New York – NIMH Community Support Program: A Position Paper and Status Report.* Albany, NY: Bureau of Demonstration Projects, New York State Office of Mental Health.

Laumann, E.; J. Galaskiewicz; and P. Marsden. 1978. "Community Structure as Interorganizational Linkages." *Annual Review of Sociology* 4:455–84.

Levine, S. 1974. "Organizational and Professional Barriers to Interagency Planning." In *A Handbook of Human Service Organizations,* edited by H. Demone and D. Harshbarger, pp. 373–80. New York: Behavioral Publications.

Levine, S., and P. White. 1961. "Exchange as a Conceptual Framework for the Study of Interorganizational Relationships." *Administrative Science Quarterly* 5(March):583–610.

Litwak, E., and L. Hylton. 1962. "Interorganizational Analysis: A Hypothesis on Coordinating Agencies." *Administrative Science Quarterly* 6(March):395–420.

Litwak, E., and J. Rothman. 1970. "Towards the Theory and Practice of Coordination Between Formal Organizations." In *Organizations and Clients,* edited by W. Rosengren and M. Lefton, pp. 137–86. Columbus, Ohio: Merrill.

Morris, R., and I. Hirsch-Lescohier. 1978. "Service Integration: Real Versus Illusory Solutions to Welfare Dilemmas." In *The Management of Human Services,* edited by R. Sarri and Y. Hasenfeld. New York: Columbia University Press.

Morrissey, J., and P. Castellani. 1981. "Interorganizational Linkages Study: Interim Progress Report." Albany, N.Y.: Special Projects Research Unit, New York State Office of Mental Health.

Morrissey, J.; R. Hall; and M. Lindsey. 1982. *Interorganizational Relations: A Sourcebook of Measures for Mental Health Programs.* DDHS Publication No. (ADM) 82–1187. National Institute of Mental Health, Series BN NO. 2. Washington, D.C.: Government Printing Office.

Mott, B. 1968. *Anatomy of a Coordinating Council.* Pittsburgh, Pa.: University of Pittsburg Press.

New York State Office of Mental Health. 1981. *Quality of Life: Evaluating the Community Support Program.* Albany, N.Y.: Bureau of Community Support Systems, New York State Office of Mental Health.

Pfeffer, J., and G. Salancik. 1978. *The External Control of Organizations: A Resource Dependence Perspective.* New York: Harper and Row.

Price, J. 1972. *Handbook of Organizational Measurement.* Lexington, Mass: D.C. Heath.

Redburn, F. 1977. "On Human Services Integration." *Public Administration Review* 37(May–June):264–69.

Riecken, H.W., and R.R. Boruch. 1974. *Social Experimentation: A Method for Planning and Evaluating Social Intervention.* New York: Academic Press.

Rieker, P.; P. Horan; and J. Morrissey. 1976. *The Structure of Interorganizational Relationships of Community Mental Health Centers: A Framework and Methods of Data Collection and Analysis.* Chapel Hill, N.C.: Social Research Section, University of North Carolina.

Sauber, S.R. 1977. "The Human Services Delivery System." *International Journal of Mental Health* 5:121–40.

Schulberg, H. 1979. "Community Support Programs: Program Evaluation and Public Policy." *American Journal of Psychiatry* 136(November): 1433–37.

Schulberg, H., and F. Baker. 1970. "The Caregiving System in Community Mental Health Programs: An Application of Open-Systems Theory." *Community Mental Health Journal* 6:437–46.

Schulberg, H., and M. Bromet. 1981. "Strategies for Evaluating the Outcome of Community Services for the Chronically Mentally Ill." *American Journal of Psychiatry* 138(July):930–35.

Steadman, H., and J. Morrissey. 1980. "Interfacing Local Jails with the Mental Health System." Albany, N.Y.: Special Projects Research Unit, New York State Office of Mental Health.

Suchman, E. 1967. *Evaluative Research.* New York: Russell Sage Foundation.

Townsend, E. 1980. *Identifying Interorganizational Clusters Within A Larger Human Services Network.* Unpublished dissertation, Graduate School of Public Administration, New York University.

Turk, H. 1977. *Organizations in Modern Life.* San Francisco, Calif: Jossey-Bass.

Van de Ven, A. 1976. "On the Nature, Formation, and Maintenance of Relations Among Organizations." *Academy of Management Review* (October):24–36.

Van de Ven, A., and D. Ferry. 1980. *Measuring and Assessing Organizations.* New York: Wiley.

Van de Ven, A.; G. Walker; and J. Liston. 1979. "Coordination Patterns Within an Interorganizational Network." *Human Relations* 32:19–36.

Warren, R. 1967. "The Interorganizational Field as a Focus for Investigation." *Administrative Science Quarterly* 12(December):396–419.

———. 1973. "Comprehensive Planning and Coordination: Some Functional Aspects." *Social Problems* 20:355–64.

Warren, R.; S. Rose; and A. Bergunder. 1974. *The Structure of Urban Reform.* Lexington, Mass: D.C. Heath.

Weiss, C.H. 1972. *Evaluation Research.* Englewood Cliffs, N.J.: Prentice-Hall.

Whetten, D. 1981. "Interorganizational Relations: A Review of the Field." *Journal of Higher Education* 52:1–28.

Zald, M. 1969. "The Structure of Society and Social Service Integration." *Social Science Quarterly* 50:557–67.

10 COMMUNITY SUPPORT PROGRAMS: Retrospect and Prospect

At this writing, mental health policy in the United States is in flux and transition, and while some of the parameters of the future are beginning to come into focus, much remains uncertain. It is increasingly clear, however, that the new federalism of the Reagan administration is leading to a radical transfer of resources, authority, and accountability from Washington to state and local governments.

In the last week in July 1981, the U.S. House and Senate completed action on the final version of the fiscal year 1982 budget. This budget eliminated approximately $35.2 billion from domestic (largely human service) programs. According to the budget, funding for about twenty federal health programs, including mental health, was consolidated into block grants to the states, with funding for these programs reduced by about $1 billion, or 25 percent. However, the National Institute of Mental Health (NIMH) Community Support Program (CSP) was not explicitly mentioned as being included in a block grant.

In the Omnibus Budget Reconciliation Act, the House of Representatives expressed interest in continuing the CSP initiative in the 1982 fiscal year and, through a Continuing Resolution, appropriated $4.8 million for state projects and $960,000 for "research related to this effort."[1] The NIMH CSP is currently providing a limited amount of continued funding, through the end of the 1982

193

fiscal year, to the eighteen states and the District of Columbia that have participated in the CSP pilot program over the last four years. In addition, CSP is providing modest grants, through the end of the fiscal year, to twenty previously unfunded states whose proposals have been reviewed by an ad hoc initial review group and approved by the National Advisory Mental Health Council.[2]

As of March 1982, however, the administration's budget request for the 1983 fiscal year did not include a specific line item for CSP. While it is possible that Congress will request funding to continue the program in the next fiscal year, the future of CSP is in question. At best, a small amount of categorical support will remain for CSP.

The decline and possible demise of specific categorical support for CSP and the simultaneous contraction of federal health, mental health, and social welfare resources during the Reagan administration are putting the CSP approach in jeopardy. The Mental Health Systems Act (MHSA), which provided a mandate for a federal-state partnership on behalf of the chronically mentally ill, has been effectively repealed. The National Plan for the Chronically Mentally Ill (NP/CMI), which was to provide a blueprint for implementing programs and initiating systemic changes, remains a draft document. Its recommendations for changes in the entitlement programs (e.g., Medicare, Medicaid, SSI) fell on deaf ears. It seems extremely unlikely that programs for chronic mental patients will flourish under current circumstances. The historical, structural, and attitudinal barriers to the humane care of the chronically mentally ill have not changed.

Nevertheless, it seems to us that the mental health service system *is* changing in an effort to be more responsive to the needs of the chronically mentally ill. Many state and local mental health agencies had been developing CSP-like community support systems (CSSs) prior to and concurrent with the NIMH program without benefit of federal categorical support. The CSS has become a generic concept; the ten components, in one form or another, have become commonplace in the mental health vocabulary. This concept and its associated philosophy has stimulated considerable activity at the state and local level—needs assessment, crisis stabilization and psychosocial rehabilitation services, and case-management programs. However, CSP is not expanding into a major mental health program, and CSP activity may soon be frozen at the federal level.

Like Camelot, CSP appears to have been "a once and future" program. What can now be said of it? What have we learned from CSP? Did it achieve its objectives? Did it generate principles and practices that can guide future reform efforts? Was it a successful model program? The ultimate question may not be whether CSP continues to exist as a federal NIMH program, but rather how far-reaching its impact has been as a program of influence.

A "ONCE AND FUTURE" PROGRAM

The NIMH CSP, the subject of this evaluation project, has not grown into a large program and is threatened with extinction, yet the need for such a program remains. In fact, current economic conditions and the limits placed on social welfare programs already may have exacerbated the plight of the chronically mentally ill in the community. If the chronically mentally ill are to be served humanely in local communities, some broad-based program similar to CSP will be needed. The chronically mentally ill and the problems created by the policies of deinstitutionalization will not magically disappear with a wave of Merlin's wand.

As of early 1982, the CSP continued to operate within NIMH, monitoring new and continuing projects, providing technical assistance, and serving as a focal point for albeit diminished federal activities on behalf of the chronically mentally ill. Some evaluation projects focusing on CSP in particular, and on the chronically mentally ill in general, continue at NIMH. However, the federal government is decreasing its direct involvement in health, mental health, and social services. With the declining federal involvement, states and local governments increasingly will be faced with fiscal and programmatic decisions about the care of deinstitutionalized patients and other chronically disabled people in the community. If, as we have suggested, a comprehensive program of services for the chronically mentally ill continues to be needed, how shall it be designed, implemented and evaluated? What generic lessons have been learned from the NIMH CSP?

At this point, we are in no position to assess the ultimate success or failure of CSP and its CSS concept. Even the planned evaluation research agenda for CSP would not have produced a definitive assessment. Most of the studies completed and reported in this volume were preliminary, hypothesis-generating, methodology development and feasibility studies. Only some of the follow-up studies necessary to evaluate CSP properly will be conducted. As noted in Chapter 1, the abrupt change in federal mental health policy presents CSP with a great challenge—a premature test of the viability of the CSS concept without substantial categorical federal support.

In a sense, CSP may have come and gone; the "once and future program" marks a phase in a limited and incomplete social reform. In this final chapter we will review the accomplishments as well as the limitations of CSP. First, we summarize what has been learned about methodology as well as about the program, its target population, and the larger system of health and social welfare services. Then, we try to assess CSP's performance in relation to its own programmatic objectives. Since this perspective may be myopic, we next turn to an external set of standards appropriate for the assessment of model programs widely regarded as "successful." Finally, we return to the broader policy significance of CSP as an incomplete social reform.

ASSESSING CSP

In spite of the limits of the initial CSP evaluation, much has been learned about the program, its clients, and the health–mental health and social welfare system in which it is embedded. An overall approach to CSP-CSS evaluation has been developed, research designs and instruments have been field tested, and baseline data have been collected. By recording this information in the present volume, we hope to inform others and to stimulate further evaluation of support systems for the chronically mentally ill. To be consistent with the order of presentation in prior chapters, the present section begins by assessing issues at the program level of analysis, and then turns to issues at the client and system levels.

Analyzing Program Logic

A major component of the federal evaluation strategy was to conduct an exploratory study called an Evaluability Assessment (EA) to identify CSP objectives, distill the logic of how these objectives were to be accomplished, and question the plausibility of key assumptions and hypotheses. The results are reported in Chapters 3 and 4.

The EA proved to be a useful process for defining program objectives and analyzing program logic. As evaluators, we found it beneficial to collaborate with program managers and staff, which was a requirement of the EA process. Broad-based agreement was established concerning the dimensions of the CSP, its goals, underlying hypotheses, and appropriate measures of program performance. As a result, the EA constituted a significant step in the development of an evaluation agenda for the future.

Monitoring Program Performance

Chapter 5 provides a detailed description of the implementation of CSP at the state level, based on field visits to nine funded states. While the data collection in the field visits was not as refined or complete as had been hoped, it nonetheless demonstrated the feasibility of monitoring program performance on a statewide basis in terms of indicators such as legislative activity, technical assistance, and interagency collaboration. One product of this study is a program-monitoring instrument with two alternative forms, incorporating different levels of detail, which can be readily used by state mental health authorities (Ben-Dashan, Morrison, and Kotler 1981). To be most useful, data on program performance should be collected longitudinally to discern changes from year to year and to probe for evidence of statewide service improvement.

The monitoring of program performance at the local level requires even more refined measures. In monitoring changes in quality of life, for example, it is necessary to assess the quality and appropriateness of available resources for meeting basic human needs, including residential arrangements, work, and recreational environments. Another example of the complexity of monitoring program performance at the local level is the assessment of cost effectiveness. As Schulberg (1979) has noted, conventional cost-accounting procedures that were developed for application in single agencies can only provide a limited basis for assessing the unit costs of CSSs. Because these community networks are so decentralized and the types of participating agencies so varied, assessments of the component and total costs of services are exceedingly complex. More comprehensive cost-accounting frameworks are clearly needed (Sorenson and Kucic 1981).

Assessing the Size and Needs of the Population

In order to plan effectively for CSSs, it is necessary to estimate the size and needs of the target population on a state and substate basis. Methods for conducting "needs-based" assessments at the state and substate levels are described in Chapter 8. These methods include community (household) surveys, surveys of community-based providers, and surveys of key informants.

Because CSPs also seek to transfer patients from institutional to community settings, data are needed to establish the size and potential needs of the institution-based target population. One approach involves conducting surveys of mental hospitals, nursing homes, and other institutional care facilities to identify those persons who are likely to be mentally and physically capable of returning to the community and to predict their demand for community support services (Chapter 8; also see Lund 1976). The method may involve surveys of a sample of residents, surveys of a sample of resident records, and/or surveys of knowledgeable care givers within the institution. Patient level-of-functioning measures and related information are then translated by clinical judgment or specified decision rules into residential placements deemed appropriate to the client population surveyed. Global judgments may also be made pertinent to other types of needed community support services.

Assessing Client Services and Outcomes

Considerable progress has been made in terms of instrument development appropriate for CSP client assessment. The Uniform

Client Data Instrument (UCDI) has been pilot tested by NIMH in eighteen different sites across the United States. Chapter 6 illustrates how such surveys can provide useful information about the social and clinical characteristics of persons served by CSSs, their current level of functioning, and the scope of services they receive. Chapter 7 shows how these same data can provide insight into factors affecting adjustment to community living.

Whereas the instrument has proven to be a useful descriptive device, it has also been limited in a variety of ways. The utilization data are not truly needs-based, and the time frame is restricted to a single month. The reliability of the subjective ratings of basic living skills, social and leisure-time activity, and behavioral problems remains to be established. Furthermore, the instrument requires additional refinement in the area of quality of life, where case-manager ratings need to be supplemented with direct client interviews (NYSOMH 1980). Some of these problems are currently being addressed in a longitudinal study by the Human Services Research Institute (HSRI).

As of this writing, we do not know very much about the clinical outcomes of CSP patients (Schulberg and Bromet 1981). Without controlled clinical trials conducted at multiple sites, it is difficult, if not impossible, to draw causal inferences about the impact these programs are having per se on the quality of clients' lives. Selection of valid comparison groups is also problematic. In lieu of assessments based on clinical outcome alone, Bachrach suggested that attention be turned to the "impact of synthesized community support systems" guided by "application of systems theory" (1981).

Assessing System Change and Impact

Chapter 9 discussed in detail the meaning and methods, as well as the promise and limitations, of systems analysis for evaluating the impact of CSP. As has been reiterated throughout this book, systems change has been a major objective of CSP. The analysis of the program logic, as well as the plausibility analysis, made clear the significance of assessing the impact of CSP in terms of an array of intermediate and long-term system changes.

The plausibility analysis, in Chapter 4, raised a variety of specific questions about CSP's involvement with the larger health and welfare system: Could a small categorical program influence the nationwide development of CSSs without additional categorical and mainstream resources? Could CSP accomplish its mission independent of the rest of the mental health and social welfare systems? Would coordination (collaboration) be possible? If so, would systems change result in improved client outcomes and quality of life? These critical questions still cannot be answered affirmatively, although Chapter 9 suggests an approach for their test and evaluation. Further research in a variety of community contexts is needed before the most significant "systems questions" can be answered.

Has CSP Been Achieving Its Objectives?

The next section of this chapter assesses CSP in terms of whether, and to what extent, the program is doing what it set out to do. The use of programmatic objectives as a yardstick for evaluation was an important component of the overall evaluation strategy (Chapter 2). If we refer to the logic model introduced in Chapter 3, we can identify CSP's major objectives and, based on the results of the short-term evaluation presented in Chapter 5, we can then assess the program's success in reaching its goals. Since the results are presented in detail in Chapter 5, we will only review the highlights below.

- *A variety of federal activities were implemented.* CSP awarded contracts, provided technical assistance to funded as well as nonfunded states, collaborated with other key federal agencies (e.g., Housing and Urban Development), and became involved in a variety of advocacy-type activities.
- In the first round of CSP program development, *every funded state established an organizational locus for the program to become a focal point for CSS development.* Not all bureaucratic locations, however, have been equally efficacious. Some programs have been successful in capturing the attention of state officials; others have floundered in administrative backwaters.

- *Each state and local program defined the target population and conducted a needs assessment.* Unfortunately, systematic efforts to characterize the needs of the target population usually focused on data descriptive of persons who were already receiving community support services. As a result, the needs assessments are mainly informative of the needs of *underserved* clients, rather than the needs of an unserved and potential clientele. Findings reported by states and local programs suggest that additional services are needed across all service categories, but that particular emphasis needs to be given to advocacy, transportation, coordination of services, and housing (Chapter 5; also see Ashbaugh, Hoff, and Bradley 1979).

- *Interagency collaboration occurred in every state* with varying results (Chapter 5; also see Ben-Dashan, Morrison, and Kotler 1981). The plausibility analysis raised some fundamental questions about the actual fruits of such coordination in spite of the many testimonies to its success. Chapter 9 reviewed some of the methodological considerations in assessing CSP's achievements on this objective.

- *Legislative activity has resulted* from efforts focused on the intermediate, systems change, objectives. Legislative activities have emphasized housing and residential issues, but expert testimony has also been provided in state legislatures in respect to a variety of other issues that concern the welfare of chronically mentally ill persons (Chapter 5; also see Ben-Dashan, Morrison, and Kotler 1981).

- *State-level technical assistance and training have also occurred.* State CSP projects now provide, coordinate, or sponsor a broad array of technical assistance and training activities. While systematic evaluations of the effectiveness of these activities are lacking, there is much anecdotal evidence to suggest that these activities have helped to develop a cadre of providers who are sensitive to the needs of chronically mentally ill persons (Chapter 5). CSP has also provided technical assistance to state and local project staff through its national and regional conferences.

- *At the local level, CSSs have been established; the ten components are in place in all demonstration sites, and clients are enrolled and receiving services* (Chapter 6). It remains to be

seen whether this activity will result in improved services and
an increase in the quality of life for chronically mentally ill
persons (Chapter 9). The plausibility analysis introduced in
Chapter 4 raised issues of attribution. Can CSP take responsibility and credit for client change or even change in the system of services? We do not know what might have developed
without CSP. Some states and local programs already had
been moving in the direction of increased attention and social
support for the chronically mentally ill prior to CSP. The attribution question remains one of the challenges of future
evaluation research.

Is CSP A Model Program?

The previous section reviewed CSP's accomplishments in terms of
the objectives around which the program defined its mission. This
section assesses CSP in relation to externally determined criteria
for evaluating "model programs," defined by Bachrach as "any
planned demonstration effort that tests the application of distinctive, often innovative, programmatic strategies to the care of
chronic mental patients" (1980: 1023).

In Bachrach's view, model programs for the chronically mentally ill should assign top priority to the most seriously disabled,
develop linkages with community resources, provide a full range
of patient care functions, and emphasize individually tailored
treatment regimens. In addition, model programs should be sensitive to the unique qualities of the communities in which they are
located, employ specially trained staff, provide access to hospital
beds in order to complement community-based services, and include an internal assessment mechanism that encourages timely
and useful feedback. Each of these principles of successful model
programs are used below as criteria for assessing the NIMH CSP.

Chronic Patients Targeted   The strength of CSP lies in its em-
bracing the chronic mental patient as its target population. Unlike its predecessors in the century-long cycles of reform, CSP
does not propose to prevent chronicity by treating early acute
cases of mental disorder. CSP is a program designed for the reha-

bilitation of chronic mental patients; it is a "network of caring" for the most seriously mentally ill.

On the other hand, CSP has selected the ambulatory chronic patient in the community as its specific target population within the larger population of chronic mentally ill persons. CSP explicitly excludes the "appropriately institutionalized" among the approximately 750,000 chronic patients in nursing homes and the 150,000 in psychiatric hospitals.[3] According to Chapter 6, case managers are almost never involved in outreach activities. Although approximately 7 percent of CSP clients have no history of hospitalization, the criteria for CSP eligibility have emphasized prior hospitalization and have given less explicit attention to the "new chronic patient," that is, the never-institutionalized, severely disturbed, young patient of the deinstitutionalization era (Pepper, Kirshner, and Ryglewicz 1981; Schwartz and Goldfinger 1981; Caton 1981; Green and Koprowski 1981; Bachrach 1982).[4]

Finally, some have warned that reliance on performance contracting invites further "creaming" of the chronic population for patients who will be most likely to improve, ensuring that performance standards will be met and contracts will be renewed (Morrissey 1982). It appears that CSP may not be immune from the "reject syndrome" (Morris and Hirsch-Lescohier 1978) which has perpetuated the neglect of responsibility for the chronically mentally ill (Gruenberg and Archer 1979).

Linkage with Other Resources   Linkage with community resources is one of the basic tenets of CSP and its concept of a CSS. Field visits to CSP sites indicated that community linkages are well developed; Chapter 5 reported on the initial assessment of these programmatic activities. Chapter 9 described how these community linkages are being measured at a CSP site in Syracuse, New York. The danger with CSP is that it could replicate the error of the community mental health center by ignoring the state mental hospital and nursing homes. In our experience, however, this has not been the case. The institutional facilities are regarded as community resources.

Functional Integrity   The full range of patient-care functions, including patients' needs for asylum, respite, socialization, and rehabilitation, are embodied in CSP's ten components of a CSS.

Chapter 6 indicated that CSP clients are receiving services in each of the ten component areas, though considerable variation exists between sites. Chapter 6 also indicated that patient-care functions are being focused on those clients who exhibit the most behavioral problems and the greatest deficits in basic living skills.

Individually Tailored Treatment   We cannot accurately verify an individual treatment approach for each client in CSP. However, we do know that case managers are familiar with their clients and report a variety of patterns of services. Certainly individualized treatment plans are expected in local CSP demonstration projects.

Cultural Relevance and Specificity   The cultural relevance of CSP is difficult to assess. Approximately 11 percent of CSP clients are nonwhite. This is only slightly less than the percentage of nonwhite persons with chronic mental disorders detected in national household surveys (Ashbaugh 1981). CSP's mandate includes a requirement to be responsive to minority needs, but no data have been collected systematically that would provide an assessment of this program's cultural relevance.

To what extent are local projects tailored to specific communities? Looking at the variety of implemented projects, one is inclined to say that the CSS model is extremely flexible. Projects have adapted to local needs and to sponsorship by a diversity of core service agencies. CSP demonstrations have begun in state mental hospitals (e.g., New York), in community mental health centers (e.g., Massachusetts and Colorado), and in psychosocial rehabilitation centers (e.g., Florida and Missouri). The ten-component model provides CSP with a broad outline within which individual projects can be innovative, adapting to local needs.

On the other hand, some communities may find the requirements of a ten-component model limiting and unnecessary in their catchment area. Just as the Community Mental Health Center Program began to find its original "five essential services" as an impediment to the proliferation of required community-based mental health services in many catchment areas, CSP might find the requirement to provide all ten components a limiting factor in the nationwide adoption of the CSS concept. Resource-poor communities may be unable to mount a complete

CSS but be desperately in need of external support to establish a partial system comprising some of the ten components. By contrast, resource-rich communities may only need "seed money" to develop a psychosocial rehabilitation and case-management program and thus complete an otherwise comprehensive CSS.

Prior to the advent of block grants, CSP guidelines were moving in the direction of facilitating project development in resource-poor as well as resource-rich communities. The MHSA had accepted the notion of funding partial community mental health center and CSS programs. The block-grant program of the Reagan administration further promotes state and local adaptation of model programs to specific needs and opportunities. The fear is that flexibility in format without guidelines will result in neglect and incomplete, inadequate services for chronic patients.

Specially Trained Staff   As part of the field test of the UCDI, some data were collected systematically on the special training of the project staff. The results from case-manager-background questionnaires administered to 211 case managers at different sites indicate that CSP staff are a mix of professional and non-professional mental health workers. Nearly two thirds of the case managers reported that they had participated in some sort of continuing education or in-service training (Bernstein 1981). Despite the fact that several state projects have developed staff-training programs, there has been little effort to evaluate the appropriateness or effectiveness of the staff training. This is a critical area for further program development as well as for evaluation research (Baker et al. 1980).

Hospital Liaison   Hospital beds are not included, per se, in a CSS. Most projects, however, satisfy the requirement for crisis stabilization with hospital beds. CSP recognizes the need for intermittent, intensive 24-hour protective interventions like acute hospitalization. In the initial version of the NIMH Definition and Guiding Principles for CSSs, mental health services were mentioned only in passing among the ten components, in a single breath along with health and dental services. A more recent version of this document, prepared in September 1980, gives greater prominence to the medical-psychiatric approach to acute crises in chronic patients. We regard the potential for excluding psychiatric practice from a CSS as inimical to chronic patients, just as the exclusion of concepts like psychosocial rehabilitation from psychiatric practice was detrimental in the past. Hospitalization or its functional equivalent must be included in a CSP project if it is to be a model program.

Internal Evaluation   As noted in Chapter 2, evaluation tasks were included in all state and local CSP projects. It was hoped that these "internal evaluations" would provide more timely feedback and be more specifically relevant to individual projects than was possible in the federal evaluation studies. While it is true that internal assessment mechanisms were in place, it is unclear whether these mechanisms actually provided timely and pertinent feedback to state and local project managers. Too often, internal evaluations were not specifically relevant to program analysis and planning and, as noted in Chapter 2, there was considerable confusion, and occasionally conflict, between federal and state-local evaluation agenda. The analysis of the needs-assessment data collected by state and local projects during their first year of program development did raise doubts about whether the data that were collected were subsequently used for program planning and policymaking (Hoff, Reday, and Bradley 1980).

CSP—An Incomplete Reform

The CSP was an important part of a needed, yet incomplete, social reform. The movement to provide humane care for the chronically mentally ill in American communities has been plagued by an absence of a clear national policy and commitment. While limited in scope, the MHSA and NP/CMI were key elements in this reform movement. Unfortunately, the near-total collapse of these federal initiatives marks a sharp reversal in the movement's momentum. With the block-grant legislation of 1981, the lack of a national policy and commitment toward the chronically mentally ill is certain to become even more apparent as decisions about whether to fund CSPs are made in fifty state capitals.

As we have noted, the core of the reform movement, of which CSP was an integral part, was regarding the chronically mentally ill as a special target population worthy of attention in its own right. Deviating from the pattern established by previous cycles of reform, the new programs were not designed exclusively to *prevent* chronic disorder. The already disabled were not to be neglected. Instead, the chronically mentally ill were accepted as a persistently disabled population in need of special habilitation and rehabilitation.

CSP was the first federal initiative devoted exclusively to improving the care of the chronically mentally ill in the community. Its influence probably exceeded its direct accomplishments. However, CSP *has* accomplished the majority of its objectives and *has* met many of the criteria of a model program. Questions still remain about the generalizability of this model and its limitations. It is not clear whether CSP's influence will continue to be felt without federal leadership and without considerable mainstream as well as categorical resource support.

CSP and its needed reform has been trapped in time by significant changes in social and economic policy. It has been caught at the crossroads between the social experiments of a generous federalism of the 1960s and 1970s and the austerity of the new federalism of the 1980s. As a result, the reform movement appears to have stalled short of its goal.

CSP was a federal pilot program, offering categorical seed money, in an era moving toward reliance on mainstream resources and state and local control over programs. Had it been implemented, the MHSA would have moved in the direction of increased program planning and fiscal responsibility at the state level. On the one hand, CSP would have become a model, a template for federally funded, state-operated programs for the chronically mentally ill mandated by the MHSA. NIMH guidelines, patterned after CSP, would have shaped these new programs. On the other hand, CSP was anachronistic. The federal mandate was weakening and many regarded the seed money concept, at least in part, a failure.

The NP/CMI had not endorsed CSP as a comprehensive solution, although CSP's influence on the plan was profound and far-reaching. The NP/CMI focused on mainstream resources, such as the entitlement programs under the Social Security Administration, and included state mental hospitals and nursing homes, children and the elderly. The NP/CMI encouraged rapprochement with medicine and psychiatry; the psychosocial rehabilitation ideology of CSP was balanced by strengthened medical-psychiatric input.

CSP signaled the new reform and figured prominently in renewed interest in the chronically mentally ill. It carried a banner at the federal level—sponsoring programs, working to change "the system", and initiating the evaluations which made this book possible. Although the definitive assessment of the effectiveness of CSP cannot yet be written, it is certain that CSP and its CSS concept *can* and *does* work. The true measure of its influence in improving the system of care and in leading to improved patient outcome will become more apparent as this decade of the "new federalism" unfolds.

The core issue of the future is not whether CSP endures as a federal program, but whether the CSP model is adopted by the states. The "old federalism" assumed that, left to their own devices, states would neglect the chronic patient. The danger is that this is exactly what will now occur, as the federal government transfers responsibility for this population to the states. On the other hand, the "new federalism" assumes that, given adequate resources, states will respond creatively to the challenge of caring in a comprehensive way for persons with chronic mental disabilities.

The problem of the chronically mentally ill remains a major mental health and social welfare challenge. The magnitude of the problem is sure to grow. Kramer (1981) notes that the prevalence of chronic mental disorder and disability is certain to increase as the large cohort of young acute and chronic patients age. Only an unlikely technological fix can reverse this trend. Without significant resources and inspired leadership, creative programs like CSP cannot succeed. With support, adequate financing, and imagination the chronically mentally ill can enjoy a reversal of a century of neglect.

NOTES

1. The total CSP appropriation for fiscal year 1982 was $1.9 million below the level appropriated in fiscal year 1981.
2. The new states to receive CSP grants include: Alaska, Delaware, Hawaii, Idaho, Iowa, Kansas, Louisiana, Mississippi, Nebraska,

New Hampshire, North Dakota, Puerto Rico, Rhode Island, Utah, Vermont, Virginia, Virgin Islands, Washington, West Virginia, and Wisconsin.

3. Estimates of the *size* of the population "appropriately institutionalized" vary. Work done for the National Plan for the Chronically Mentally Ill estimated that two-thirds of the institutionalized population are "appropriately placed" in long-term care facilities.

4. New CSP eligibility guidelines attempt to include these "new chronic patients."

REFERENCES

Ashbaugh, J.W. 1981. "Preliminary Estimates of the Size and Selected Characteristics of the Adult Chronically and Severely Mentally Ill Population Living in U.S. Households." Boston, Mass.: Human Services Research Institute.

Ashbaugh, J.W.; M.K. Hoff; and V. Bradley. 1979. "Community Support Program Needs Assessment Project: A Review of the Findings in the State CSP Reports and Literature." Boston, Mass.: Human Services Research Institute.

Bachrach, L.L. 1980. "Overview: Model Programs for Chronic Mental Patients." *American Journal of Psychiatry* 137, no. 9: 1023–31.

————. 1982. "Young Adult Chronic Patients: An Analytical Review of the Literature," *Hospital and Community Psychiatry* 33, no. 3 (March): 189–197.

————. In Press. "Assessment of Outcomes in Community Support Systems: Results, Problems and Limitations." *Schizophrenia Bulletin.*

Baker, F.; J. Intagliata; R. Kirshstein; and N. Crosby. 1980. "Case Management Evaluation Phase One Final Report Vol. 1, CSS Clients, Services, Staff, Program Impact." Buffalo, N.Y.: Tefco Services, Inc.

Ben-Dashan, T.; L. Morrison; and M. Kotler. 1981. "Community Support Program Performance Measurement System Development and Short-Term Evaluation Final Report." Silver Spring, Md.: Macro Systems, Inc.

Bernstein, A.G. 1981. "Case Managers: Who Are They and Are They Making Any Difference in Mental Health Service Delivery?" Unpublished Ph.D Dissertation, University of Georgia.

Caton, C.L.M. 1981. "The New Chronic Patient and the System of Community Care." *Hospital and Community Psychiatry* 32, no. 7: 475–78.

Green, R.S., and P.F. Koprowski. 1981. "The Chronic Patient with a Nonpsychotic Diagnosis." *Hospital and Community Psychiatry* 32, no. 7: 479–81.

Gruenberg, E., and J. Archer. 1979. "Abandonment of Responsibility for the Seriously Mentally Ill." *Milbank Memorial Fund Quarterly/ Health and Society* 57:485–506.

Hoff, M.K.; M. Reday; and V.J. Bradley. 1980. "Community Support Program Needs Assessment Project: A Review of the Use of Needs Assessment Information in State CSP Reports." Boston Mass.: Human Services Research Institute.

Kramer, M. 1981. "The Increasing Prevalence of Mental Disorder." Paper presented at Langley Porter Institute, San Francisco, Calif., August 6.

Lund, D.A. 1976. "Appropriateness of Level of Care: The Pilgram Project." Albany, N.Y.: Bureau of Program Evaluation, Department of Mental Hygiene.

Morris, R., and I. Hirsch-Lescohier. 1978. "Service Integration: Real Versus Illusory Solutions to Welfare Dilemmas." In *The Management of Human Services*, edited by S. Sarri and Y. Hasenfeld, pp. 21–50. New York: Columbia University Press.

Morrissey, J.P. 1982. "Deinstitutionalizing the Mentally Ill: Processes, Outcomes, and New Directions." Forthcoming. In *Deviance and Mental Illness, edited by Walter Gove. Sage Annual Reviews of Studies in Deviance,* Vol. 6. Beverly Hills, California: Sage Publications.

New York State Office of Mental Health, 1980. "Quality of Life: Evaluating the Community Support Program." Albany, N.Y.: Bureau of Community Support Systems.

Pepper, B. M.C. Kirshner, and H. Ryglewicz. 1981. "The Young Adult Chronic Patient: Overview of a Population." *Hospital and Community Psychiatry* 32, no. 7: 463–69.

Schulberg, H.C. 1979. "Community Support Programs: Program Evaluation and Public Policy." *American Journal of Psychiatry* 136, no. 11 (November): 1433–37.

Schulberg, H.C., and E. Bromet. 1981. "Strategies for Evaluating the Outcome of Community Services for the Chronically Mentally Ill." *American Journal of Psychiatry* 138, no. 7 (July): 930–35.

Schwartz, S.R., and S.M. Goldfinger. 1981. "The New Chronic Patient: Clinical Characteristics of an Emerging Subgroup." *Hospital and Community Psychiatry* 32, no. 7: 470–74.

Sorenson, J.E., and A.R. Kucic. 1981. "Assessing the Cost Outcomes and Cost Effectiveness of Community Support Programs (CSP): A Feasibility Study." Unpublished paper, University of Denver. Denver, Colorado.

INDEX

211

About the Authors

Richard C. Tessler is on the sociology faculty at the University of Massachusetts in Amherst. Much of the research for *The Chronically Mentally Ill: Assessing Community Support Programs* stems from a temporary assignment to the National Institute of Mental Health during 1979–1980 where he coordinated community support program evaluation activities and also contributed to the National Plan for the Chronically Mentally Ill. He is the author or co-author of numerous articles in medical sociology and mental health and is currently an associate editor of the *Journal of Health and Social Behavior*.

Howard H. Goldman of the Langley Porter Psychiatric Institute is currently director of medical student education for the Department of Psychiatry at the University of California in San Francisco. As a research psychiatrist at the National Institute of Mental Health during 1978–1980, Dr. Goldman provided extensive consultation to the community support program and assumed a major role in the development of the National Plan for the Chronically Mentally Ill. He is co-author, with Joseph Morrissey and Lorraine Klerman, of *The Enduring Asylum*. In addition to his numerous teaching activities, Dr. Goldman continues to investigate the efficacy and delivery of mental health services.

219

LIST OF ASSOCIATES

John W. Ashbaugh
Vice President
Human Services Research
  Institute
120 Milk Street
Boston, Massachusetts

Tal Ben-Dashan
Macro Systems, Inc.
8630 Fenton Street
Suite 300
Silver Spring, Maryland

Alice G. Bernstein, Ph.D.
Social Science Analyst
Institute of Program
  Evaluation
General Accounting Office
Washington, D.C.

Martin Kotler
Chairman of the Board
Macro Systems, Inc.
8630 Fenton Street
Suite 300
Silver Spring, Maryland

Ronald W. Manderscheid, Ph.D.
Acting Chief
Survey and Reports Branch
Division of Biometry &
  Epidemiology
National Institute of Mental
  Health
Rockville, Maryland

Lanny Morrison
Macro Systems, Inc.
8630 Fenton Street
Suite 300
Silver Spring, Maryland

Joseph P. Morrissey, Ph.D.
Senior Research Scientist
Special Projects Research
  Unit
New York State Office of
  Mental Health
44 Holland Avenue
Albany, New York

Phyllis Rienzo
Macro Systems, Inc.
8630 Fenton Street
Suite 300
Silver Spring, Maryland

Beatrice M. Rosen
Mental Health Consultant
11702 College View Drive
Wheaton, Maryland

Beth Stroul
Macro Systems, Inc.
8630 Fenton Street
Suite 300
Silver Spring, Maryland